SPORTS STARS WITH HEART

Kevin Garnett
ALL-STAR ON AND OFF THE COURT

by J Chris Roselius

PURCHASED WITH
TITLE V FUNDS

Enslow Publishers, Inc.
40 Industrial Road
Box 398
Berkeley Heights, NJ 07922
USA
http://www.enslow.com

Library of Congress Cataloging-in-Publication Data
Roselius, J Chris.
  Kevin Garnett : all-star on and off the court / by J Chris Roselius.
    p. cm. — (Sports stars with heart)
  Includes bibliographical references and index.
  ISBN-13: 978-0-7660-2863-0
  ISBN-10: 0-7660-2863-1
  1. Garnett, Kevin, 1976—Juvenile literature. 2. Basketball players—United
States—Biography—Juvenile literature. 3. Minnesota Timberwolves
(Basketball team)—Juvenile literature. I. Title.
  GV884.G3R67 2007
  796.323092—dc22
    [B]   2006031921

Credits
Editorial Direction: Red Line Editorial, Inc. (Bob Temple)
Editor: Sue Green
Design and Page Production: The Design Lab

Printed in the United States of America

10 9 8 7 6 5 4 3 2 1

To Our Readers: We have done our best to make sure all Internet
addresses in this book were active and appropriate when we went to press.
However, the author and the publisher have no control over and assume no
liability for the material available on those Internet sites or on other Web
sites they may link to. Any comments or suggestions can be sent by e-mail
to comments@enslow.com or to the address on the back cover.

Photographs © 2007: AP Images: 14, 20; AP Photo/Paul Battaglia: 78; AP
Photo/Rick Bowmer: 42; AP Photo/Duane Burleson: 77; AP PHOTO/Aaron Harris:
13; AP Photo/Ann Heisenfelt: 3, 4, 29, 34, 44, 63, 83, 105; AP Photo/Bill Janscha:
56; AP Photo/Kim D. Johnson: 94; AP Photo/Andy King: 3, 10, 107; AP Photo/Jim
Mone: 53, 66; AP Photo/Lucy Nicholson: 1; AP Photo/Tom Olmscheid: 91; AP
Photo/Rich Pedroncelli: 70; AP Photo/Mustafa Quraishi: 84; AP Photo/Tom
Strattman: 3, 22; AP Photo/Scott Troyanos: 47; AP Photo/David Zalubowski: 102

Cover Photo: Kevin Garnett gets past a defender in a game against the Los
Angeles Clippers April 13, 2002.

CONTENTS

Blazing a Trail, 5

Growing Up in South Carolina, 17

Leaving for Chicago, 28

Adjusting to the NBA, 37

Leading the Wolves to the Postseason, 50

Garnett Makes History Again, 61

Picking Up the Pieces, 72

Establishing Himself On and Off the Court, 82

Reaching New Heights, 90

A Leader and a Giver, 100

Career Statistics, 112
Career Achievements, 114
Chapter Notes, 115
Glossary, 121
For More Information, 122
Index, 123

Kevin Garnett is named the NBA's MVP in 2004.

CHAPTER ONE

Blazing **1** a Trail

Kevin Garnett is a National Basketball Association (NBA) Most Valuable Player (MVP), winning the award in 2004. He also earned an Olympic gold medal for the United States at the 2000 Summer Games in Sydney, Australia. Garnett's legacy, however, is always going to be linked to what he did in 1995.

Standing in front of a multitude of media members after his high school senior season at Farragut Academy in Chicago, Garnett became the first player in two decades to declare himself eligible for the NBA Draft straight out of high school. His decision—and success in the NBA—led other high school basketball players, such as Kobe Bryant, Tracy McGrady, Jermaine O'Neal, and LeBron James to declare themselves eligible for the draft in the following years.

In high school, Garnett was a man playing among boys. He scored 2,533 points, grabbed 1,807 rebounds, and blocked 739 shots during the course of his four-year career. As a senior at Farragut Academy, he averaged 25.2 points, 17.9 rebounds, 6.7 assists, and 6.5 blocked shots per game to lead Farragut to a 28–2 record and the Class AA state quarterfinals.

Postseason awards were showered upon Garnett once the season was done. He was named the National High School Player of the Year by *USA Today* and was

KEVIN GARNETT'S HIGH SCHOOL CAREER

His Senior Year

Year	Average	Rebounds	Blocked shots	Assists
1994–95	25.2	17.9	6.5	6.7

His Entire High School Career

Year	Points	Rebounds	Blocked shots
1991–95	2,533	1,807	739

selected to the *Parade Magazine* All-America Team. He also earned the honor of being named Mr. Basketball for the state of Illinois.

Garnett's dominance on the court continued during the spring. Playing against the top high school players in the nation at the 1995 McDonald's All-America Game, Garnett showed he could compete against the best. He ran the floor with the grace of a gazelle and showed off a variety of offensive and defensive skills. He won the Wooden Award, named after legendary coach John Wooden, as the Most Outstanding Player after racking up 18 points, 11 rebounds, 4 assists, and 3 blocked shots to lead his West squad to a 126–115 victory.

Watching Garnett's every move on the court was Wooden, as well as a host of NBA scouts. They all wanted to see what Garnett could do in person. He did not let them down, despite the pressure of being so carefully observed.

DID YOU KNOW?
Kevin Garnett was named Mr. Basketball in two states. He garnered the honor in South Carolina, where he starred for Mauldin High School. He moved to Chicago before his senior season and was named Mr. Basketball for the state of Illinois in 1995.

"I didn't put any pressure on myself," Garnett said. "I am not going out there to put on a show. If they like what they see, fine. If they don't, I am not going to change anything. I'm just going to work harder."[1]

WEIGHING HIS OPTIONS

After graduation, Garnett, a six-foot eleven-inch forward, was not sure he wanted to jump straight to the NBA. He was interested in attending college. There was only one problem—he was having trouble scoring high enough on the SAT and ACT tests to be eligible to play in college.

> **"I know I will be among the finest players in the world."**
>
> **—Kevin Garnett**

Garnett had taken the ACT three times. Each time he had fallen one point short of the seventeen needed to be able to play as a freshman in college. Retaking the ACT and SAT once again was an option. He had been working hard on improving his test scores. He was even enrolled in a class designed to improve his test-taking skills.

But the clock was ticking. The deadline for entering the NBA Draft was rapidly approaching.

Garnett decided to hire agent Eric Fleisher to help guide him through this difficult period in his life. Garnett was being compared to Moses Malone, a Hall of Famer who leapt straight from high school to the American Basketball Association. In 1974, a nineteen-year-old Malone had signed with the Utah Stars.

Soon, it was time for Garnett to make a decision. He could wait and learn what his test scores would be and possibly miss the draft deadline, or he could declare himself eligible for the draft. About a week after his nineteenth birthday, Garnett held a press conference. He announced his decision to enter the draft. Weeks later, after he was drafted, Garnett learned he scored high enough on the SAT to be eligible to play in college.

In a letter to NBA commisioner David Stern, Garnett wrote, "I am prepared for this great endeavor. I know I will be among the finest players in the world."[2]

The decision to enter the draft was not an easy one for Garnett. His mother, Shirley, always stressed the importance of a good education. But Shirley was raising Garnett and his two sisters on her own and often had to work two jobs.

Garnett wanted to please his mother and get an education. But he also knew millions of dollars were awaiting him if he turned pro. With that money, he would be able to take care of his family, which he loved.

Only three players—Malone, Darryl Dawkins, and Bill Willoughby—had made the jump directly from

Garnett shoots over the Lakers' Karl Malone.

high school to the NBA. Garnett took advice from a variety of people. In the end, he decided to head to the NBA, following the advice given to him by Willoughby.

"I told him, 'Don't let anybody tell you what's best for Kevin Garnett,'" Willoughby said.[3]

Garnett could have followed the lead of Magic Johnson, who had enough talent to go pro after high school but still went to college. However, Garnett chose to do what was best for him and his family.

"I didn't really look at everybody else. I did what I had to do for myself," Garnett said. "I didn't take Kareem or Magic Johnson into account— no disrespect intended to them. When you do something, you have to look at it from your own perspective, your own view, and I was confident when I did it."[4]

PRESS RIPS DECISION

For twenty years, a route to the NBA had been established. After playing high school basketball, a player attended college to improve his skills before entering the NBA. Garnett's decision to skip college was not greeted with cheers and high fives, at least not by those in the media.

Around the country, journalists wrote their opinions about Garnett and his choice. Most of the opinions were not very flattering toward Garnett.

"First of all, Kevin Garnett is not ready to play in the NBA. He just isn't close," wrote Michael Wilbon of the *Washington Post.* "We're going to assume his coach simply hasn't seen enough NBA games, live, up-close. The kid isn't physically ready to play under the basket in the Big Ten, much less against Hakeem Olajuwon and David Robinson. His skill level isn't high enough; he isn't savvy enough."[5]

Jay Mariotti of the *Chicago Sun-Times* was not much kinder in his view of Garnett's decision.

"Is Kevin Garnett ready for it all? Obviously, hell, no," Mariotti

> "When you do something, you have to look at it from your own perspective, your own view, and I was confident when I did it."
>
> —Kevin Garnett

11

wrote. "It is such a fragile proposition—the thought someone could enter the NBA so young, no matter how gifted and tall and extraordinarily athletic, and be better off in the long term. The years after high school are perhaps the most crucial in human development, particularly for a basketball phenom, who should grow socially and scholastically in college while refining raw skills in the gym against peers. In the pros? He grows up in airports and Hyatts, trying to learn the big time during rare practices in a whirlwind season, assuming the team isn't so rotten that skill growth is impossible."[6]

Even NBA executives were not quite sure about Garnett's decision to try to take on the NBA and the best players in the world. Yes, he displayed amazing grace on the court. He could leap out of the building and already possessed a soft, feathery shooting touch, allowing him to play all over the offensive end of the court.

Garnett also displayed the physical skills needed to survive in the NBA. He could send opponents' shots back down the court with brute force. He could block out defenders and grab nearly every available rebound. But he was doing all of that against fellow high school opponents, not even college opponents.

That was a concern among NBA executives.

"You're rolling the dice even with college players in the draft, but at least they have established a learning curve," said Rob Babcock of drafting a high school athlete. At the time, Babcock was serving as the Minnesota Timberwolves' director of player personnel. "You're really rolling the dice with high school kids."[7]

OPINIONS START TO CHANGE

While members of the media and some NBA executives had their opinions about Garnett, he changed many of their minds

Toronto Raptors general manager Rob Babcock speaks at a 2004 news conference.

after they watched his private workouts.

Babcock was one of those wowed by what Garnett was able to do on the court. Garnett showed off his nifty ballhandling skills and shooting range. Babcock was overwhelmed by Garnett's ability to play as if he was a guard instead of a six-foot eleven-inch forward.

Babcock described Garnett's workout as the "most impressive individual workout I've ever seen."[8]

Garnett easily handled the ball up and down the court. He fired off pinpoint passes normally thrown only by point guards.

His shooting range had not been seen before. He was able to play with his back to the basket and showed off a variety of post moves. He could also bounce outside near the three-point line and launch jump shot after jump shot.

Babcock wasn't the only member of the Minnesota organization who was impressed with Garnett's skills. Flip Saunders was the general manager who would later become Garnett's head coach with the Timberwolves. After watching Garnett run through a series of drills during a workout, Saunders probably summed Garnett up best.

Garnett decided to skip college and make the leap from high school right to the NBA.

"He has the running ability and agility of a (six-foot two-inch) player," Saunders said.[9]

Veteran NBA coach Doug Collins described Garnett as "a genetic freak. All the great ones are."[10]

At first, the Timberwolves planned to try using Garnett as a decoy. The Timberwolves wanted the four teams drafting ahead of them to take a long look at Garnett. Saunders and Kevin McHale, the Timberwolves' vice president of basketball operations, planned to talk up the amazing high school athlete and say how much they would love to have him. They hoped the stir they created would lead one of the four teams to select Garnett, leaving a more experienced college player for the Timberwolves to choose.

However, that plan quickly changed when McHale and Saunders fell in love with Garnett. They instantly knew Garnett was the player they wanted to build the franchise around.

> "... a genetic freak. All the great ones are."
>
> —Doug Collins describing Garnett

"We were gonna say how much we liked him after we watched him work out," Saunders said. But after watching Garnett work out, Saunders said, "I turned to McHale and said, 'We ain't telling anybody anything.'"[11]

On the day of the draft, everyone was nervous. Garnett

was wondering where he would be selected. His workouts erased doubts about his skills. Yet there were still doubts about his maturity. It had been twenty years since someone so young had entered the NBA. Would he be able to make the adjustment to the professional game?

The Timberwolves were also worried. They did not know what the four teams selecting in front of them were going to do. The waiting finally came to an end when, after the first four selections were made, Garnett was still available. Minnesota wasted no time in selecting the teenager.

The team had a star in the making, one they could make the centerpiece of the team for years. Garnett quickly gained the love of the Minnesota fans as well as his teammates. He soon took to his nickname—Da Kid.

Already known around the country from his high school days, Garnett was used to the stardom and adoration he received from fans during his rookie season in the NBA. But the bright lights of the league were a far cry from his childhood days in South Carolina.

2 Growing Up in South Carolina

Kevin Garnett was born attached to a baskeball. Well, that wasn't really true. But it probably seemed that way to anyone who knew him when he was growing up. Whenever possible, Kevin was playing the game he loved.

Thump. Thump. Thump. That was the sound neighbors heard while Kevin dribbled the ball. Swish. Swish. Swish. That was the sound of his constant jumpers. It didn't matter what the time was. Kevin played basketball whenever possible.

"All he did was talk about basketball," said childhood friend Baron Franks. "And every time you saw him, he had a ball. Sun up. Sun down. Up and down the street. All day long.

"This is a guy who would lay down at 3 A.M. and then be up at 9 A.M. to play ball. He would think everyone else had to get up, too. And whoever did get up to play with him played all day. I mean, I liked basketball, too. But not like he did."[1]

Born on May 19, 1976, in Greenville, South Carolina, Kevin did not grow up with his biological father, O'Lewis McCullough. Kevin's mother, Shirley Garnett, did her best to raise Kevin, his older sister, Sonya, and his younger sister, Ashley.

Shirley worked two jobs to make ends meet. She also received child support payments from McCullough, who had remarried and started a new family. When Kevin was five years old, his mother married Ernest Irby. But Irby was not the father figure Kevin hoped to find. Instead, the two were often at odds.

"Me and my stepfather didn't get along," Kevin said. "I'd say, 'Why don't you put a goal up?' He'd say, 'You don't need no goal.' My mom was easily influenced. After a while, I just had to be disobedient."[2]

Kevin's disobedience was nothing too terrible, however. He stayed away from drinking and taking drugs. While he did get into minor trouble for petty vandalism and staying out late, he was usually very responsible. He had to be.

His mother stressed hard work and getting an education. Kevin did the best he could to live up to her expectations and help take care of his younger sister. As a teenager, he earned money bagging groceries and cleaning restrooms at restaurants. He was not afraid to work hard. In fact, it was something he felt he had to do.

"I've always had a job," Kevin said. "In all fairness to myself, I had no choice but to be responsible. I had to. I had to work, you know? And I've had some jobs in my life. More than a couple. I had no choice. I've always had to find some way to help out somebody that I found myself being responsible for."[3]

> **DID YOU KNOW?**
> Kevin says his favorite meal is breakfast because it helps him stay alert throughout the day.

Shirley didn't support Kevin's decision to play basketball until he was a junior in high school and was a rising star.

"I'm an advocate of education, always saved for my children's college educations," she said. "My plans were for him to go to school. He's positive, loves people and believes in giving. I think he would have made a great social worker."[4]

Kevin Garnett was chosen by the Minnesota Timberwolves in the 1995 NBA Draft.

Being responsible was a part of Kevin's nature. However, he needed something of his own. He played some football as well as basketball. But when he wanted to get away, to be the boy he really was, he always turned to basketball, which he started to play while in elementary school. The game was his best friend and allowed him a place to find safety.

"When I didn't have a friend, when I was lonely, I always knew I could grab that orange pill and go hoop," Kevin said. "If things weren't going right, I could make a basket and feel better."[5]

MAULDIN OFFERS CHANCE TO DEVELOP

His love and skill for basketball came from McCullough. If there was one gift McCullough passed on to his son, it was the ability to play basketball. At Beck High School in the 1970s, McCullough was a gifted and talented hoops player.

The captain of the basketball team, he earned the nickname "Bye Bye 45" for his ability to blow past fellow defenders, leaving them only a glimpse of the 45 he wore on the back of his uniform. His playing days were long over by the time Kevin started to play, but McCullough's ability was passed along.

However, McCullough was not a constant figure in Kevin's life. His stepfather did not encourage him to play the game he loved so much. Often, Kevin's basketball games consisted of him playing against himself, though he did have some friends to play with as well.

> **"If things weren't going right, I could make a basket and feel better."**
>
> **—Kevin Garnett**

Garnett goes for the slam over the Indiana Pacers' defenders.

At the age of twelve, Kevin and his family moved to Mauldin, which is about ten miles southeast of Greenville. His mother believed it offered a safer place for Kevin and his sisters to grow up. Mauldin also offered something to Kevin he did not have in Greenville—a group of people who shared his passion for basketball.

One of those friends was Jamie "Bug" Peters. Jamie and Kevin grew so close to each other that they often told people they were brothers. They are still close today. Jamie quickly saw Kevin had talent on the basketball court. He encouraged his new friend as much as possible.

Jamie did not play basketball, but he was always providing the support Kevin needed in order to improve. He even talked Kevin into sneaking out of his house and heading to Springfield Park to work on his game while Jamie watched.

Another friend was Baron Franks. Baron was five years older than Kevin. He described the future MVP of the NBA as "a lanky kid with no skills" when he first saw Kevin play.

But Kevin started to take basketball seriously. He was set on improving his skills. If he were to play in college and eventually the NBA, he needed to play better—and older—competition. Baron provided that for him.

On the court, Baron was not Kevin's friend. He was his mentor. Baron did all he could to make Kevin better and tougher. He taught Kevin that basketball was not an easy game to play.

"I didn't do him no favors," Baron said. "I gave him all I had. And sometimes, I'd take a rebound and bounce it off his head or something. And I gave him a lot of noise. I'd tell him, 'I'm in control, controlling the game. I have you in my pocket.'"[6]

Kevin never shied away from the tough competition. Facing taller opponents, he was forced to develop his outside game, skills that he still uses in the NBA today. Kevin also had to work on his dribbling skills in order to get around the larger opponents he was facing.

Playing against opponents such as Baron allowed Kevin to grow rapidly on the court.

"I remember one day, at the park, when the guys were saying he was 6-feet-6 and couldn't dunk," Baron said. "But every year, he improved dramatically . . .

"He was always looking for a father figure to tell him about basketball, and that's how he bonded with us older guys."[7]

BECOMING A HIGH SCHOOL STAR

While Kevin was learning basketball on the blacktops of Mauldin, he did not officially play organized basketball until his freshman year of high school. He was still raw, and he was still gangly out on the court.

But he could play.

"I knew he was gifted the first time I saw him on the court," said James Fisher, who was Kevin's high school coach.[8]

Kevin excelled on defense. Taking advantage of his height and quick feet, he averaged 14 rebounds per game and 7 blocked shots. He did not assert himself on offense as much as he could have. He felt as much joy passing the ball as he did scoring. Fisher said he was amazed that Kevin did not care who scored the points as long as his team won the game. Even with his unselfish play, Kevin still averaged 12.5 points per game.

As was the case on the playground, Kevin worked tirelessly in the gym. He took whatever Fisher threw at him during practice. Nothing was too hard for Kevin to handle.

"I'd bust him at basketball practice, I mean really bust him," Fisher said. "And then he'd go to the park and play basketball there. He'd leave one practice and go practice again. I never saw someone so obsessed."[9]

REMEMBERING AN OLD FRIEND

After moving to Mauldin from Greenville, Kevin made friends with a variety of people, many of whom shared his passion for playing basketball.

One of his friends was Eldrick Leamon, a power forward who played with Kevin on the same AAU team. In 1994, Eldrick was killed in a traffic accident, leaving a void in Kevin's life. To this day, Kevin remembers Eldrick before every game.

During team introductions, amid the wild cheers and pregame festivities, Kevin sits on the bench, to the right of an empty chair. Kevin puts his elbows on his knees, clasps his hands, and bows his head. Why does he do this? He is remembering his fallen friend.

"I always envision him sitting right there next to me. That's why I keep the last seat open. I get into this mode that I can't even explain because when I get into it, I don't see anything. I'm in my own little world. The only time I come out of it is when the game is over."

After the high school basketball season ended, Kevin played for an Amateur Athletic Union (AAU) team coached by Darren "Bull" Gazaway. Playing with and against the best players during the summer, Kevin continued to improve his game.

When he was a sophomore, Kevin's game reached a new level. All of the hard work he put in on the court at the park or in the gym produced an all-around player with magnificent skills.

"I don't think I ever saw a kid enjoy playing that much," said Stan Hopkins, Mauldin's athletics director. "When you have that kind of talent and work ethic, it turns you into a super player."[10]

Despite his height, he moved with catlike reflexes on the court. He seemed more like a guard than a power forward or center. He could hit the outside shot if opponents packed the paint with defenders. When given the chance to take on a defender one-on-one, he was able to play with his back to the basket and display a variety of post moves.

He could also start the fast break with a quick outlet pass to a guard streaking up of the court or finish the break with a thunderous dunk after sprinting down the floor past opposing players. At Mauldin and for his AAU team, Kevin was becoming a star. However, he made sure his teammates were along for the ride.

"Kevin could have averaged 30 points a game—easy," Gazaway said. "But he didn't. He probably averaged about 18 points (for his AAU team). He would pass, set up other players. He was not stingy. Just loved to play the game."[11]

College scouts were coming from near and far to watch Kevin play, both at his high school and at his AAU games. His name was becoming well known around the country. He was invited to play at Nike summer camps in Indiana, Oregon, and Illinois.

DID YOU KNOW?
One of Kevin's nicknames is "Da Kid." Though he is now a veteran NBA player, he is still a kid at heart. During his spare time, Kevin loves to play video games, especially Navy Seal on PlayStation 2 and Ghost Recon on Xbox. He also likes to spend time with his family and relax as much as possible.

Kevin flourished during his junior season. Taking on more responsibility on offense, he averaged 27 points per game. Defensively, he was still a force to be reckoned with as he grabbed 17 rebounds and blocked 7 shots per game. While playing, he was always smiling and laughing with his friends.

Everything was going well. Mauldin advanced to the state championship game. Kevin was named South Carolina's Mr. Basketball, the first junior in state history to receive the honor. Everyone was sure that Mauldin was set to win the state title in Kevin's senior season.

But the Mavericks never got that chance.

CHAPTER THREE

Leaving for Chicago

Despite the good times on the court, Kevin's mother always worried about her little boy. She knew he wasn't getting into major trouble, but she also knew that everything was not perfect in Mauldin.

The town was small and offered little in entertainment. That forced teenagers to try to find their own entertainment. But what happened in May of 1994 was never expected and changed everything for Kevin.

Kevin enjoyed a spectacular junior season. Fans could not wait to see what he was going to do for Mauldin as a senior. But Kevin would never play at Mauldin High School as a senior. By the time the basketball season rolled around, he was living in Chicago and attending Farragut Academy.

Kevin rarely talks about what happened in May 1994. When he does refer to it, he calls it "the incident in Mauldin." One day a white student was beaten at the school. Several versions of what happened have been reported. The truth remains hidden somewhere amid all the stories.

What cannot be denied is the fact that Kevin and four others were blamed for what happened to the white student. Kevin was arrested and charged with second-degree lynching. The arrest made headlines in all of the papers in the area and around the state.

Garnett sits on the bench during a game against Golden State.

Kevin maintained his innocence from the beginning of the ordeal. Several witnesses said Kevin was just an innocent bystander. He just happened to be in the wrong place at the wrong time. Others said the white student was known as a troublemaker. That did not change the fact that Kevin was arrested.

"Just knowing Kevin like I do, I don't think he ever would do anything to hurt anyone, and I never understood why the whole thing was made such a big deal," said Murray Long, one of Kevin's teammates at Mauldin. Murray, a white student, was one year older. "When someone told me Kevin was arrested—for lynching—I kind of laughed. I just didn't believe it."[1]

Kevin learned a valuable lesson about stardom during his ordeal. Because of his fame, people were attracted to him like iron to a magnet.

During his darkest moment as a teenager, he found out who his real friends were. Friends such as Jamie Peters remained. Jamie was there for Kevin no matter what happened in the past. He was not about to leave his best friend alone now.

But many other people Kevin considered friends did not stick around like Jamie did.

"At the time I thought I had amps of friends," Kevin said. "I thought everybody was my boy. When you get in trouble, or you go broke, that's when you find out who your boys are. You know what I'm saying?

"When you get in trouble, you see all the

FINDING TIME TO RELAX

The NBA season is long and grueling, often leaving players too exhausted to do anything on their days off. Kevin often spends his off days at his home playing video games. During the off-season, however, he likes to travel to different countries and meet new people. When not traveling, he enjoys spending time with his friends and family.

masks come off. You've got something like basketball or a nice job, people always want to be around you. Once you mess up? They're gone. Because they're fronts. A lot of fronts out there, man—that's what I learned."[2]

Kevin also learned that being who he was—the star basketball player who was destined for greatness—he had to be aware of his surroundings at all times. He couldn't just do something and worry about the consequences later. His days of innocence were over after "the incident."

"I'm a wiser Kevin, a smarter Kevin, a more mature Kevin," he said nearly a year after his arrest. "After the incident happened, I calmed myself, I settled myself. It was a wake-up call."[3]

NEW CITY, NEW CONTROVERSY

Because Kevin had never been in trouble before, he qualified for a pretrial intervention program for first-time offenders. Eventually, the charges were dropped. However, for Kevin and his family, the damage had already been done.

Throughout the whole ordeal, Shirley Garnett was not happy with what happened. She felt the school administration did not support her son as much as it should have. With the entire incident covered by the media, Kevin's reputation had been damaged.

Shirley decided it was time to get out of Mauldin and start again. By September, she had moved the family to Chicago. Their new neighborhood was completely different from the one they had left.

"I had to save him," Shirley said of her son.[4]

Kevin's enrollment at Farragut, however, did not go unnoticed. The coach at Farragut was William Nelson. A couple of years earlier, Nelson had been a coach at a Nike camp and had been assigned to Kevin.

He got to see how Kevin lifted his teammates and made them better. During that one week at camp, Kevin's team won 13 of the 14 games it played. When news broke that Kevin was at Farragut, allegations arose in the media that Nelson recruited Kevin. Nelson has always denied the charges.

Other media members alleged that Nelson was receiving money from Nike, the shoe company, or that Nike was helping Kevin's family with its moving and living expenses.

If that was the case, why did Kevin's family pay $700 per month to live in a one-bedroom apartment? Shirley worked two jobs to provide for her family in a city where the cost of living was much higher than in Mauldin.

"It was hard, very hard—to eat rice many

DID YOU KNOW?

When growing up in South Carolina, Kevin was a big fan of the Los Angeles Lakers. His allegiance changed to the Bulls when he moved to Chicago before his senior year in high school.

nights, to go to the grocery store and realize you have only $20 on your Visa, having to walk when my car was stolen several times," Shirley said. "I cried many nights."[5]

Meanwhile, Kevin was struggling in the classroom. As hard as he tried, he failed to score high enough on his college entrance exams. Soon, word about those failures leaked out.

DID YOU KNOW?

Kevin's favorite movie is *Scarface*, and his favorite actor is Al Pacino.

Just as happened back in Mauldin, a private moment in Kevin's life was soon public knowledge.

"That hurt Kevin," Shirley said. "That hurt him deeply. It was one of the most horrible experiences a young man can go through."[6]

IMMERSED IN BASKETBALL

Gangs plagued the neighborhood where the Garnetts lived. They were surrounded by more crime and more drugs than they had been in Mauldin. Kevin's closest friends had been left behind when he moved. Now, in Chicago, his every move seemed to be debated by everyone. Kevin turned to basketball more than ever. It was his escape.

As a basketball player, Kevin was at his best. Despite having to adjust to new teammates and different opponents, he averaged 25.2 points, 17.9

Garnett heads toward the basket in a game his rookie season.

rebounds, 6.7 assists, and 6.5 blocked shots per game. The team advanced to the Class AA state quarterfinals and ended the season 28–2.

If there was one problem with Kevin during his senior year at Farragut, it was that he was perhaps too unselfish. He was able to dominate any opponent guarding him on the floor. Basically, no one could stop him.

But Kevin did not want to be Mr. Superstar. He wanted to be a good teammate. He would pass the ball to his teammates and try to get them involved in the game, even if it would have been better for him to shoot in certain situations.

Kevin's coach at Farragut, William Nelson, did not press his players too often. He wanted them to enjoy playing basketball and the time spent on the court with their teammates. But even he would get frustrated with Kevin's decisions on the court at times.

DID YOU KNOW?

While on vacation in Hawaii, Kevin decided to do something he had never done before. Standing on a cliff in Maui, he leapt off the edge and dropped 25 to 30 feet before landing in the water below.

"I'd be there yelling, 'Kevin don't pass—shoot, shoot!'" Nelson said.[7]

It was his unselfishness, however, that drew the attention of NBA scouts. Kevin showed that he was not a one-dimensional player who only cared about scoring. Instead, he showed an enthusiasm to get his teammates involved on the court, to make them feel as if they were important members of the team.

His willingness to pass and not just shoot was one of the many reasons why the Minnesota Timberwolves selected him with the fifth overall pick in the NBA Draft and made him the cornerstone of their franchise.

MAN OF INFLUENCE

Kevin quickly made a name for himself in the NBA, proving he was a talented player on the court during his very first season. But he also proved to be powerful away from the court. In its April 21, 1997, edition, *Newsweek* named Kevin one of the 100 most influential people of the decade.

Despite all the adversity surrounding his move to Chicago, Kevin believes it made him a better player. Being in Chicago prepared him for the NBA.

"A lot of people don't know it, but you have to be a gladiator to play (high school ball) in Chicago," he said. "It's like a mini-NBA, and I have the scars to prove it."[8]

CHAPTER FOUR

Adjusting to the NBA

Entering his first season in the NBA, Garnett was not a normal rookie. Everyone—the media, fans, other NBA players, and executives from around the league—was watching every move Garnett made.

He was not just a rookie. He was an experiment. There were no other players his age, and it had been two decades since anyone tried to make the transition from high school to the NBA.

"He's been blessed with a terrible thing—potential," McHale said. "A lot of guys have 'potential' written on their gravestones. Spent their whole life with that potential. The thing about potential is, you've got to realize it.

"If you don't, you're a wash. You could have a very good NBA career, but with the potential he has, you would be classified as a washout. He's a kid who has to live up to that potential."[1]

If Garnett failed, it would prove to all of his critics that he should have gone to college, not only to work on his skills, but to mature mentally. If he failed, the future wave of high school players jumping to the NBA would likely never have happened.

In order to reach the potential McHale was talking about, Garnett needed to answer two main questions surrounding his first professional season. Was he going to be ready physically? Was he mentally able to handle life in the NBA?

MORE THAN MENTALLY READY

Within months after being drafted by Minnesota, Garnett was a millionaire. His first professional

THE RUBBER-BAND MAN

As a high school student in Mauldin, South Carolina, Kevin Garnett and his family did not have a lot of money. Many of Garnett's classmates wore jewelry, a luxury Garnett could not afford. So, he used rubber bands as a substitute, saying the idea just came from the concept of doing something different that he could call his own. To this day, Garnett wears rubber bands and says they offer a little sense of security and a little extra boost. When he does something wrong on the court, he often snaps himself with the bands as a way of telling himself to snap out of it.

contract paid him $5.6 million over three years. Without a doubt, Garnett enjoyed his newfound wealth. He lived in a nice apartment and later a house. He drove a new car and watched television on a giant screen.

Everything he was unable to have growing up was now available to him. But Garnett was not going to let money change who he really was.

"It's real nice. It has some rich parts," Garnett said when describing the area in which he lived. "Of course, I'm not rich or anything. Well, I wasn't.

"See, that's the funny thing. I don't feel like I have a lot of money. I live every day like I'm poor." Garnett believes you should not change your life "just because you have a few million dollars in your pocket."[2]

But instant wealth was just one of the hurdles that Garnett had to clear as a rookie. The constant presence of media and fans presented a challenge, too. Before being drafted, he was on the cover of *Sports Illustrated*. Throughout his high school career, he was constantly in the press, especially after the incident in Mauldin and his following move to Chicago.

DID YOU KNOW?
Before entering the NBA, Kevin graced the cover of *Sports Illustrated* on June 26, 1995, under the title of "Ready or Not . . .".

Wherever Garnett went, someone was sure to be there ready to ask a question or seek an autograph or just a minute of his time. At times, the wear and tear of being in the public eye placed a strain on Garnett, especially before the start of the season.

Most often, people wanted Garnett to explain himself. That is tough enough for mature adults to do, much less someone who is nineteen. After hearing the same questions again and again, he would simply answer, "I'm different from most nineteen-year-olds."[3]

Soon, Garnett realized that this was to be his life in the NBA. He quickly learned he was going to constantly be in the spotlight and that he would be asked the same question again and again as he traveled from city to city. He rapidly adjusted his style and started handling the interviews with ease and grace. Garnett was even mindful of his teammates, often asking reporters to respect the space of fellow players while crowding around his locker.

Garnett made sure to engage the public as well. Always willing to give, Garnett spoke at local schools during his spare time, telling students about the virtues of an education.

Because Garnett was new to Minnesota, some of the students did not

NOW THAT IS GOOD FOOD

Garnett likes to eat a lot of different kinds of healthy food. But he says his favorite foods are still hamburgers, french fries, and pizza.

know who he was. But when a six-foot eleven-inch man stands up to speak, students listen. At one middle school, Garnett told the students that what they were learning that day was going to be with them for the rest of their lives.

Being around the children allowed Garnett to be the child he still was. Before or after games, he often talked with children while sporting a big smile on his face. He would get on their level and be a kid himself before signing an autograph or giving away a pair of shoes.

At the middle school, Garnett knew that many of the students he talked to probably had brothers who were his age. Garnett always likes to have fun and enjoy his surroundings, and that is the advice he often gives to middle school students.

> **"You go through middle school once in your life, so you might as well enjoy it."**
>
> **—Kevin Garnett**

"You go through middle school once in your life, so you might as well enjoy it," Garnett says. "It's like this NBA thing. When it's over, it's over. I can't say, 'Well, I should have done this, I should have done that.' You've got to have fun with it, so you can remember the good times."[4]

Garnett shoots over Miami's
Keith Askins.

But Garnett was not going through mental challenges only away from the court. There were challenges on the court every night he played. Players from around the league were not about to take it easy on Garnett, a teenager who was trying to push his way into the exclusive men's club called the NBA.

When challenged on the court, Garnett could have backed away, but that would have shown he was weak and not ready to battle with the veterans of the league. Instead, Garnett battled back, demanding he be respected as much as any other NBA player.

"I'm not going to let my age determine whether I get bullied around or not," he said. "Just because I'm learning doesn't mean I'm going to lay down and bow down. You're not gonna just talk to me and turn away. I'm still a basketball player, I'm still going by my playground rules. You know what I'm sayin'? It's a form of disrespect. I just try to let them know I'm out there playin' ball, and I'm not gonna take (it)."[5]

DID YOU KNOW?

Garnett has a tattoo of his initials "K.G." and another of an arm holding a basketball with the words "Blood, Sweat and Tears."

PROVING HIMSELF PHYSICALLY READY

Garnett showed throughout the season that he was mentally prepared to take on the NBA. However, showing he was physically ready came in spurts. His first challenge was breaking into the starting lineup.

Garnett reaches to block a shot by Miami's Billy Owens on October 28, 1995.

For the first time in his life, he was being used off the bench. He often entered games to give forwards Christian Laettner and Tom Gugliotta a rest.

Garnett's age was a big reason why he was coming off the bench. His versatility may have held him back as well. Minnesota could not really decide what position he played.

"Kevin Garnett is not a small forward, he's not a forward, he's not a center," McHale said. "He's a basketball player."[6]

Garnett instantly showed his ability to play against fellow NBA players. In the Timberwolves' home opener, Garnett came off the bench to score 8 points and grab 5 rebounds. He also had fans talking after a pair of jaw-dropping blocked shots. Despite the fact one of the blocked shots was ruled goaltending, fans watching the replay on the scoreboard inside the arena gasped in amazement at what they had just witnessed. Each game would provide a glimpse of what Garnett could do on the court.

During a November game against the Vancouver (now Memphis) Grizzlies, Garnett demonstrated how he could lift his teammates and his franchise onto his shoulders. Struggling against the Grizzlies, Garnett gave his team a spark in one quick sequence of events.

Grabbing a defensive rebound, Garnett quickly found a teammate and whipped a pass up the court. He didn't stop there. He immediately sprinted down the court, flying past smaller, supposedly quicker guards and forwards. When he reached the top of the three-point line, Garnett received a pass, stopped, and without a moment of hesitation, launched a shot. It swished through the net. That play awoke the Timberwolves as they went on to beat the Grizzlies by 23 points.

As the season progressed, each night seemed to bring a different highlight from Garnett. One night he made a great alley-oop pass from out of bounds. On another night, he created a fast break dunk by threading a pass between two defenders. He followed that with a no-look pass to a teammate for a basket. Each night featured another amazing moment.

NBA PLAYER OR ACTOR? Given the chance to be in a movie, Garnett portrayed a young Wilt Chamberlain in the 1996 film *Rebound*.

After a few months, it became clear to everyone how valuable Garnett was to his team. The Timberwolves realized he needed to be a bigger part of it, and others from the league recognized that fact as well.

"He has great instincts, and it looks like he has great passion for the game," said Tony DiLeo, Philadelphia's director of scouting. "Those are two ingredients for being a great player. He can score around the basket. He can go outside and hit a jump shot. He can block shots. He's definitely special—for a high school player to step into the NBA and do a lot of good things on the court, he has to be."[7]

Garnett blocks the Suns'
Wesley Person.

Able to guard smaller players thanks to his quickness, Garnett was not always able to use that speed on offense. He was not used to having to create his own shot away from the basket.

He also struggled to take advantage of his height. He was not strong enough to establish position in the paint. Because he was often weaker than his opponents, Garnett was unable to attack the basket. Proof of that was the fact he took only 66 free throws in his first 48 games as a pro.

There was one other problem. He had not yet realized he needed to establish himself on offense.

"He is a tremendously unselfish kid. Maybe to a fault," McHale said. "We say to him, 'Sometimes, Kevin, if you have a mismatch, we need you to go ahead and take your guy.' That'll come. I couldn't be happier with what Kevin's done."[8]

> **"My first year was tremendously tough."**
>
> **—Kevin Garnett**

BREAKING INTO THE STARTING LINEUP

Despite the flashes of brilliance and increased leadership Garnett was displaying when he stepped on the court, the team was going through some turmoil. For every win it earned, the team was losing two games. The losses were taking a toll on Garnett.

"My first year was tremendously tough," he said. "I'm someone who loves-loves-loves to be winning."[9]

McHale realized changes had to be made. Coach Bill Blair was fired and replaced with Flip Saunders, who was the team's general manager. Saunders wanted to hand the keys of the franchise to Garnett. That eventually meant the departure of Laettner, who was traded.

"He's the one guy who has the attitude that we can get it done down the stretch," Saunders said of Garnett. "At nineteen, he's almost our leader . . . . He's our future. He has to play."[10]

With Laettner gone, Garnett stepped into the starting lineup and flourished. Averaging nearly 6 points and 4 rebounds per game for most of the first half of the season, Garnett took advantage of his increased playing time in the second half.

Garnett ended the year averaging 10.4 points and 6.3 rebounds per game. His 1.6 blocks per game set a club record. His strong finish earned a spot on the NBA All-Rookie Second Team. While Minnesota finished the year 26–56, the record was the second best in franchise history.

By the end of the year, Garnett had proven all of the skeptics wrong. More important, he was ready to lead the team to heights it had never reached before.

CHAPTER FIVE

Leading the Wolves to the Postseason

During the off-season, Garnett returned to South Carolina to be with his friends. Whenever the sounds of squeaking shoes and basketballs being dribbled were heard at the Mauldin recreation center, there was a good chance Garnett was there playing basketball with the local high school boys.

Garnett did not just play basketball with them. He took care of them and mentored them. After games, he would often take eight or more players out to eat, teaching them how to make good food choices. He explained to them the importance of a good diet, of eating vegetables and drinking juice, not soda.

When the meal was done, the storytelling would begin. One player after another asked Garnett what it was like to play against Michael Jordan and all of the other top players in the NBA.

The people of Mauldin knew how important Garnett was to the community. In August 1996, nearly three hundred residents honored Garnett with a dinner. Each table was decorated with a photo of Garnett, and he was awarded a key to the city. During a halftime ceremony at a football game later that fall, the number 21 he wore at Mauldin was retired.

GOT MILK?

Garnett has appeared in a variety of commercials during his career, including ads for the American Dairy Association's "Got milk?" campaign.

HE SAID IT

"It's always fun to play Mike. He's not old enough to be my dad, I don't think. . . . I always call him my big brother. He's always been there for me, whenever I needed advice. You'd seen Magic and you'd seen Larry, but Michael opened up the doors for America to really see the personalities and go behind the scenes. For all he's done for the game, for all he's done for myself and my family, I've always given much appreciation and awe."

—Kevin Garnett talking about Michael Jordan after the two went head-to-head for the last time in a regular season game in January 2003. The Timberwolves won the game in Washington.

With the help of Nike, Garnett was able to resurface Springfield Park, the place where he had spent days and nights practicing and improving his skills.

"He comes back here and really pulls together the community," said Charles Bankhead, the father of C.W. Bankhead, a Mauldin High basketball player Kevin nicknamed "The Future."[1]

IMPROVEMENT IN MINNESOTA

At the end of the 1995–96 season, McHale and Saunders knew Garnett was going to be a player the team could build around. The lanky teenager proved himself during his rookie season, and there was no reason to believe that he would not improve.

They also knew that to win more games, they needed more than one superstar. Garnett needed to

THE "OBF"

Garnett often says he does not have a lot of friends, but the few he has are a group who have been loyal to him since his childhood. A small group of those friends and family members are known as the "OBF" or "Official Block Family." They help run Garnett's business affairs and provide him a support system. Garnett said the "OBF" consists of about twenty people.

Joe Smith (left), Stephon Marbury (center), and Kevin Garnett pose for photographers on picture day January 25, 1999, in Minneapolis.

be surrounded with talent. Having Gugliotta was a good start, but the Timberwolves felt they needed one more player. That player turned out to be point guard Stephon Marbury.

After a fantastic freshman season at Georgia Tech, Marbury declared himself eligible for the 1996 NBA Draft. On the day of the draft, McHale worked out a deal that landed Marbury in Minnesota. Marbury's arrival gave the Timberwolves a point guard who could get the ball to Garnett. In addition, Marbury was able to hit the three-point shot, which created more room inside for Garnett.

The addition of Marbury to the tandem of Garnett and Gugliotta worked out well for the Timberwolves. In fact, the team had its best season ever in 1996–97. It won a franchise-best 40 games and made the postseason for the first time in team history.

With teams having to concentrate on Garnett, Gugliotta was the leading scorer for Minnesota. He averaged 20.6 points per game and an impressive 8.7 rebounds. Marbury stepped in and averaged 15.8 points and 7.8 assists per game.

Then there was Garnett. He quickly became one of the top forwards in the league. During the off-season, he added more muscle to his frame. This enabled him to better handle the opposing power forwards and centers

THE KEY TO SUCCESS

Garnett is blessed with natural ability, but he knows a person cannot rely on ability alone. The key to success, according to Garnett, is having a strong work ethic. He believes having a work ethic and setting goals are very important. Success, he said, is not about making money or attaining materialistic desires. Success is setting a goal and achieving it.

who sometimes guarded him. Garnett improved greatly from his rookie season. He increased his points per game to 17.0 while grabbing an average of 8.0 rebounds. Defensively, he proved he was a force in the paint. He broke his own record for blocks per game, averaging 2.1, which led all forwards in the NBA.

Garnett's improved play was noticed around the league. At the age of twenty, he became the youngest All-Star in NBA history since Magic Johnson. In the All-Star Game, he scored 6 points and grabbed a team-high 9 rebounds in 18 minutes of action. During the season, opponents often designed their defenses to stop Garnett, sending two or three defenders at him.

Showing how well he knew the game, Garnett did not force the action during the season. When he was double-teamed, he quickly found the open player and passed to him. Garnett sacrificed his game in order for his team to win.

"He could be the world's biggest jerk if he wanted to," Gugliotta said, "but he's a pleasure to play with."[2]

AS GARNETT GOES, SO GO THE TIMBERWOLVES

While Gugliotta and Marbury were important pieces to the Minnesota puzzle, Garnett was the player who held everything together. When Garnett played well, the Timberwolves won. When he struggled, the team also struggled.

Garnett dunks in front of Dallas Mavericks forward
Samaki Walker on January 17, 1998.

In the opening two months of the season, Minnesota started slowly. The team went 12–18, including a 5–10 record during December, a month in which Garnett missed five games due to an ankle injury.

In November, when the Timberwolves went 7–8 on the court, Garnett averaged 15 points per game with an impressive 9.4 rebounds. His numbers dropped in December to 14.8 points and 8.0 rebounds per game. It was no coincidence that the team struggled as Garnett struggled.

Those struggles disappeared in January and February, the two best months of the season for both Minnesota and Garnett. In January, when the Wolves won 9 of the 15 games they played, Garnett scored 19.3 points per game, his best average of any month that season. He also averaged 6.8 rebounds.

Garnett topped 20 points in 7 games, including twice scoring 30 or more points. With Marbury and Gugliotta also producing on the court, the Timberwolves were establishing themselves as a postseason threat, something they had never done in the history of the franchise.

"These guys play unselfish ball," McHale said. "They think of themselves as basketball players, not quasi-entertainers. One guy has a bigger game one night, the other isn't upset."[3]

The good times continued in February. Minnesota won 8 of its 11 games. Again, Garnett was at his best, scoring 18 points per game and grabbing 8.2 rebounds. Three times he had a double-double. He fell just one rebound short of chalking up a fourth double-double.

But Garnett slumped in March, averaging only 17.1 points and 7.7 rebounds per game. His drop in production corresponded to a drop in wins for the Timberwolves, who lost 10 of their 16 games.

The March swoon put Minnesota's chances of making the playoffs in jeopardy. With ten games remaining, the Wolves needed some wins to secure a spot. Like Superman coming out of a telephone booth, Garnett jumped into action to help save the team's season.

During the first two games of the month, Garnett was at his best. There was Garnett throwing down a powerful dunk, punctuating a fast break basket. Soft jumpers from the wing were added to short jump hooks in the paint. A flurry of offensive moves yielded basket after basket as he scored 24 points in a 94–89 win against New Jersey.

Against Washington two nights later, Garnett picked up where he left off against the Nets. The Wizards had no answer for Garnett as he poured in 22 points to lift the Timberwolves to a 97–95 victory and a three-game winning streak.

As the playoff push continued, Garnett did

DID YOU KNOW?
In only his second season in the league (1996–97), Garnett helped Minnesota, which joined the NBA as an expansion franchise in 1989, to its first playoff berth. The next season, Garnett led the Timberwolves to their first winning record.

his best to lead his team to its first-ever postseason berth. He followed the opening two games of the month with outings of 13, 20, and 19 points. The next contest, he tallied 21 points, a game in which he also had 15 rebounds.

After the 21-point, 15-rebound game, Garnett came back strong with a 16-point, 15-rebound outing to lead Minnesota to a 95–87 victory against Dallas. Minnesota finished the season by winning one of its last three games, but that win against Milwaukee secured a spot for the Timberwolves in the playoffs as the sixth seed in the Western Conference.

PLAYOFF HYSTERIA ENDS QUICKLY

Minnesota fans were thrilled as the regular season closed. For the first time in team history, the Timberwolves were going to play a postseason game. There was only one problem. Their first-round opponent was the Houston Rockets, winners of the NBA title in 1994 and 1995. The Rockets were loaded with experienced players who had succeeded in the playoffs before.

Leading the Rockets was Hakeem Olajuwon, the NBA Finals MVP in 1994 and 1995. Also playing for Houston were veterans Charles Barkley, Clyde Drexler, Mario Elie, and Kevin Willis. In all, the Rockets had nine players on the roster who had played a combined 644 postseason games.

Minnesota had a total of 131 games of playoff experience among four players. Garnett and Marbury were barely out of their teens and would have been finishing their sophomore seasons if they were in college.

The mismatch on paper played out on the court. The Rockets swept Minnesota out of the playoffs in three games. Houston won the first game 112–95 and the second game 96–84 before closing out the series with a 125–120 victory.

But Garnett proved he could handle the bright lights of the postseason. In the opening game, Garnett poured in 21 points while grabbing 9 rebounds and dishing out 4 assists. In the second game of the series, Garnett did all he could, scoring 14 points while ripping down 12 rebounds, but it was not enough.

The Timberwolves stayed close for much of the third game. Entering the fourth quarter, the two teams were tied. But Garnett, who finished with 17 points and 7 rebounds, was unable to lift Minnesota past the more experienced Rockets. Houston pulled away down the stretch to end the Timberwolves' season.

Losing in the first round of the playoffs was disappointing, but Timberwolves fans were hoping for better things in the future. Garnett was quickly becoming a superstar. Marbury and Gugliotta were not far behind. The team boasted three great players and plenty of hope for more success in the years to come.

CHAPTER SIX

Garnett Makes History Again

After Garnett showed vast improvement from his rookie season, the Minnesota Timberwolves felt certain he was going to be a superstar. Under NBA rules, the team was allowed to offer a contract extension to their star and lock him for years to come.

Minnesota had to decide if it wanted to pay for the right to keep Garnett in a Timberwolves uniform past the 1997–98 season. Team management offered a six-year, $102 million extension to Garnett. Much to their surprise, Garnett turned down the offer, stunning nearly everyone who follows the NBA.

Garnett's agent, Eric Fleisher, was certain his client would be able to command more money on the free agent market after the season. It was a tense time for fans in Minnesota. Would the Timberwolves increase their offer? Or was there a chance they would let Garnett become a free agent after the season and try to sign him then?

Minnesota was on the clock to get something done before the October 1 deadline. Realizing how important Garnett was to the community, not just the franchise, owner Glen Taylor increased his offer. Eventually, Garnett agreed to a history-making six-year, $126 million extension. At the time, the deal was the largest multiyear contract in professional sports.

Shaquille O'Neal's $120 million, seven-year deal with the Los Angeles Lakers was previously the most lucrative long-term contract.

"Minnesota is my home," Garnett said at a news conference announcing the deal. "We've got a bright future in Minnesota. I want to play for this team, and I like Kevin McHale."[1]

Once again, like so many other times in his life, Garnett was thrust into the role of villain. First, it was his decision to bypass college for the NBA. Now, some critics were nasty in their remarks about his new contract. They called Garnett the poster boy for greed.

BREAKING THE BANK

Garnett made history when, at the young age of twenty-two, he signed the biggest sports contract in history, agreeing to a six-year, $126 million deal.

Garnett talks with reporters during the Timberwolves' media day October 2, 1997, at the Target Center in Minneapolis.

In reality, Garnett was only haggling for a larger contract because that was part of doing business in the NBA. Garnett did not want to leave Minneapolis. He had become a part of the community. But he also knew others around the league would love to have him on their teams.

"It wasn't a money issue with me," he said. "If it was, I would have told everybody to save their time so I could go through free agency and test the market."[2]

GETTING READY FOR THE SEASON

With Garnett's contract sealed, the team was able to focus its attention on getting ready for the 1997–98 season. Coming off their first playoff appearance, the Timberwolves were no longer a league laughingstock. Teams from around the NBA were no longer chalking up Minnesota as an easy win—not with Garnett, Gugliotta, and Marbury running the show.

"We're going to have to be a different team because we had success," backup point guard Terry Porter said. "Our opponents are going to look at us differently. Our days of sneaking up on people are over. I don't think it will be 'We got Minnesota, it's going to be an easy game' anymore."[3]

But there was still a question of just how good Minnesota was. During the 1996–97 season, Minnesota struggled against the top teams in the league. The Timberwolves won just 8 of 38 games when they faced teams with winning percentages of .500 or better. Against teams that were below .500, the Wolves were 32–12.

With Garnett leading the way, Minnesota set out to prove it could beat any team in the NBA.

BREAKOUT YEAR

With the baggage of owning the largest contract in professional sports, Garnett could have crumpled under the expectations everyone had of him. Instead of falling like a house of cards, Garnett came through with the best season of his young career.

He was stronger than ever, yet just as quick and talented on both ends of the floor as he ever had been. Garnett was able to dominate opponents like never before. He scored in double figures in all 82 games for the first time in his career. Posting up in the paint or shooting midrange jumpers, Garnett could not be stopped.

ONE TOUGH DEFENDER

In back-to-back games in January 1997, Garnett blocked a career-high 8 shots. He swatted away 8 shots on January 3 against Boston and again the next night against Milwaukee.

Garnett's workload on offense increased after the loss of Gugliotta to an injury halfway through the year. Garnett scored more than 20 points 31 times. In a March 29 game against Sacramento, Garnett scored a season-high 32 and added 14 rebounds and 6 assists in a 104–96 victory. Garnett ended the year with a career-high average of 18.5 points.

Where Garnett really improved was in his rebounding and playmaking skills. Garnett established new career highs in rebounds and assists, averaging 9.6 boards and 4.2 assists per game. Forty-three times Garnett recorded a double-double. Garnett also averaged 1.8 blocks per game, making him an all-around force for the Timberwolves.

"This is a person more than seven feet tall who is quicker than you are," said teammate Sam Mitchell.

Garnett holds onto the rim after a first-half slam dunk against the Golden State Warriors on January 12, 1998.

"I play against him every day in practice, and unless all my tricks are working, I can't even get my shot off. You have to beat him by three steps because if you beat him by one or two he will come up behind you and block your shot."[4]

Without question, Garnett's best game of the season came on January 3 against Denver. Cutting through the Nuggets' defense, Garnett sank 6 of his 10 shots and all 6 of his free throws to pile up 18 points. He worked hard in the paint, ripping down 13 boards—5 offensive and 8 defensive. More impressive was his running of the offense.

SO, WHO IS THE TOUGHER MATCHUP?
Garnett said the NBA is stocked with talented players, but there are a few who give him a particularly tough time. One of them is Tim Duncan. Garnett said Duncan is tough to defend because of all the moves he has. Garnett said Chris Webber is also difficult to defend. But perhaps the toughest player to defend is Rasheed Wallace. Garnett said Wallace is able to run fast, jump high, and has a good shooting range.

Wanting to get his teammates involved in the offense, Garnett split pairs of defenders or threw passes over them. He dished out 10 assists to end the night with his first career triple-double. Garnett also threw in 3 blocked shots to round out his evening.

Garnett's outstanding game sparked a 10–3 run the rest of the month. The Wolves carried a 25–18 record heading into February and were on track for another playoff berth and the franchise's first winning season. But after winning only five games in February and winning only three of its first ten games in March, the Timberwolves were 33–33 with only sixteen games remaining.

Thanks in large part to Garnett, the Timberwolves won five of their last six games in March and went on to win seven of their ten games in April to end the year with a franchise-best 45–37 record.

READY FOR SEATTLE

In April, with the season on the line, Garnett was at his best. He averaged 20.8 points and 11.0 rebounds, his best figures of any month that season. With Garnett playing at his finest and Minnesota riding a streak of twelve wins in sixteen games, Wolves fans felt the team was ready to claim its first playoff series victory.

Minnesota entered the playoffs as the No. 7 seed in the Western Conference. The seeding meant the Wolves had to face Seattle, the second-best team in the conference.

In the first game of the series, the Sonics controlled the tempo from start to finish en route to a 108–83 victory. The Wolves then made history on April 26 when they defeated Seattle 98–93 for the team's

DID YOU KNOW?

During the 1998–99 season, Garnett ranked among the NBA's top twenty in scoring (eleventh), rebounding (ninth), and blocked shots (thirteenth).

first playoff victory. Garnett scored 13 of his 15 points in the second half and had 8 rebounds to help Minnesota claim the win.

Seattle tied the game, 86–86, with a little more than four minutes remaining. Garnett gave the Wolves a two-point lead with 3:02 remaining when he scored after hustling for a loose ball.

"Even with three fouls, I knew I had to be more aggressive yet cautious," Garnett said. "When I saw open spots, I tried to take advantage of them. And when I saw loose balls, I tried to get them up as quick as possible."[5]

With the series heading to Minnesota, the Timberwolves held the home-court advantage in Game 3. They did not disappoint their fans. Claiming a 98–90 victory, the Wolves took a one-game lead in the series. Again, Garnett played a pivotal role in the victory. He scored 19 points and grabbed a team-high 8 rebounds while handing out 6 assists and blocking 3 shots.

Trailing by five points heading into the fourth quarter, Minnesota outscored Seattle by 13 in the final 12 minutes to claim the victory. Not surprisingly, Garnett was in the middle of the action.

"We rode K.G. in the fourth quarter," Marbury said. "Anthony Peeler played great and shot the ball well. Seattle played their best ball tonight, but we just wanted it more."[6]

Garnett goes for a layup against the Kings.

During a two-minute span in the fourth quarter, Garnett was at his best. Outjumping everyone around him, Garnett snared an offensive rebound and dunked the ball for an 85–78 lead with 5:06 remaining. Hustling down the court on Minnesota's next possession, Garnett lost his defender and nailed an eight-foot jumper. His teammates then found him open for a ten-foot jumper to give the Timberwolves a commanding 93–78 lead with 2:59 left in the game.

"I don't really remember how I did it," Garnett said of his fourth-quarter heroics. "All I know was the crowd was crazy. When I saw opportunities, I took the shots. In the first half I was too anxious and excited."[7]

Minnesota had a chance to wrap up the series at home and advance to the second round. But

Seattle came out strong in Game 4 and claimed a 28–21 lead at the end of the first quarter. The Sonics held on to defeat Minnesota 92–88 despite Garnett's 20 points and 10 rebounds. The loss meant the series was headed back to Seattle, where the Sonics would have home-court advantage.

Back in Seattle, the Sonics proved too much for the Timberwolves. Seattle cruised to a 97–84 win, outscoring Minnesota by 16 points in the second half. For one of the few times in his life, Garnett was unable to come through for his teammates.

The cornerstone of the franchise struggled all night, scoring only 7 points, all in the first half, on 3-of-11 shooting. Garnett managed to grab only 4 rebounds and suffered an uncharacteristic 10 turnovers.

Garnett was upset after the game. He felt he did not come through when he was needed most by his team. As is often the case with Garnett, however, he used the game as a learning experience instead of letting it defeat him personally.

> **DID YOU KNOW?**
>
> **Garnett was selected to represent USA Basketball at the 1998 FIBA Men's World Championship July 29 through August 9, 1998, in Athens, Greece.**

"What did I learn from this?" Garnett said. "I learned that sometimes you can get too hyped up. You can be too emotional. I think patience is important."[8]

CHAPTER SEVEN

Picking Up the Pieces

Garnett suffered through a long off-season after the loss to Seattle, an off-season that lasted four months longer than normal. The start of the 1998–99 season did not begin until January 1999 due to a lockout. NBA owners blamed the lockout in large part to Garnett's large contract.

By the time the season started, the Timberwolves were suddenly a team in transition. Minnesota had to watch Gugliotta take his scoring punch and walk away as a free agent. Then came problems with Marbury.

A superstar in the making, Marbury was going to want a giant contract. However, there was no chance Marbury was ever going to make what Garnett was earning. The Timberwolves decided to act early and traded Marbury to the New Jersey Nets only eighteen games into the season. In a matter of months, Minnesota went from a team that won 45 games and nearly advanced to the second round of the playoffs, to a club that seemingly was rebuilding around its superstar.

The Timberwolves, however, were not without talent. Joe Smith, the former top pick in the 1995 NBA Draft, was added. The trade of Marbury to the Nets brought Terrell Brandon, a playmaker who could hit the outside shot. And, of course, Garnett was still on the team. Knowing he had to do more, Garnett averaged a team-leading 20.8 points and 10.4 rebounds, the first time in his career he averaged a double-double for a season.

Minnesota started quickly, winning eight of its first ten games. On April 5, the club owned a 20–13 record. But the Wolves struggled the rest of the month and ended the year with a 25–25 record, making the playoffs for a third straight season. And for the third straight season, Minnesota was knocked out in the first round, this time by San Antonio, in four games.

During the off-season, Garnett played for Team USA in the 1999 Tournament of Americas, a qualifying tournament for the 2000 Sydney Olympics. Surrounded by All-Stars, Garnett and Team USA rolled through the tournament to earn a spot in the Olympics.

The experience of playing for his country was something Garnett said he thoroughly enjoyed. He

DID YOU KNOW?
Garnett went on a tour of England, Italy, and Spain during the summer of 2001 to promote basketball and his business interests.

saw the tournament as an honor and a way to have fun while playing with some of the best players in the world. Playing with his typical enthusiasm and embracing the local community, Garnett was one of the most popular American players in Puerto Rico, where the tournament was held.

"Some guys look at it like work," Garnett said. "At least when I went, it was fun. We were not only competing against each other, we were having fun. We understood we needed to be respectful, and there were certain times we had to do some stuff. But we were there to have fun, too.

"I think the Puerto Rico trip was great. I'll never forget that. We had Gary Payton and Timmy (Duncan) and a lot of great guys. It was cool. We had chemistry. For us, we were family. We all went out."[1]

PLAYOFF BLUES CONTINUE

Entering the 1999–2000 season, Garnett felt the team was ready to get over the playoff hump. Brandon was now fully acquainted with Garnett and the Minnesota system. The Wolves also drafted forward Wally Szczerbiak, a player who would add instant offense and take some of the pressure off Garnett.

However, Minnesota was struggling to find the right mix on the court and won only seven of its first twenty games. Then, two things occurred that sparked the Timberwolves.

First, Saunders inserted Malik Sealy, Garnett's idol growing up and now his best friend on the team, into the starting lineup. Sealy fit in perfectly with Garnett. At the same time, Garnett simply decided to dominate on the court.

Facing Dallas on December 18, Garnett was an unstoppable force. He spun in the paint for a dunk. He came around a screen, stopped, and hit an open jumper. Defending the basket as a knight defends his castle, Garnett swatted away or altered shot after shot. Simply put, Garnett did whatever he wanted. He scored 27 points on 11-of-18 shooting, while ripping down 14 rebounds, handing out 5 assists, blocking 2 shots, and hitting one of his 2 three-point attempts.

The Garnett "Tour de Force" continued for the next four games. Garnett scorched Cleveland for 24 points, 18 rebounds, 4 assists, and 3 blocked shots. Chicago offered no resistance as "Da Kid" racked up 22 points, 13 rebounds, 4 assists, one block, and one three-pointer. Even more impressive was all three of the games came on the road, with Minnesota winning each game.

Back in Minnesota for one game, Garnett put on a show for the home fans. He poured in 23 points against Seattle and added 14 rebounds, 6 assists, and

A BIG READER

Since childhood, Garnett has always been a big reader. He used to love the Ramona book series when he was younger. His favorite author, even today, is Beverly Cleary.

4 blocked shots. Then came a history-making performance against Orlando on December 27. Garnett scored 26 points and snatched a franchise-record 23 rebounds. Garnett was acting like a point guard, racking up 7 assists and one three-pointer. He also added 4 blocked shots.

That week of play was Garnett's finest stretch up to that point of his career, earning him Player of the Week honors. Seeing the season spiraling out of control, he placed the Timberwolves on his back and led them on a five-game winning streak to turn the year around.

Garnett finished with his best season yet as a professional. He set career highs in average points scored (22.9), rebounds (11.8), and assists (5.0). Garnett became just the ninth player in league history to average at least 20 points, 10 rebounds, and 5 assists. Garnett even made 37 percent of his shots from behind the three-point line.

For the second season in a row, Garnett started for the Western Conference in the All-Star Game. He continued his amazing play with 24 points, 10 rebounds, and 5 assists.

Minnesota went on to win a franchise-record 50 games and entered the playoffs with an air of confidence it never experienced before. But once again,

Garnett drives against Detroit's Ben Wallace in the second half of a game played on December 15, 2000.

the season came to a sudden close earlier than anticipated. Portland eliminated the Wolves in four games, despite Garnett averaging 18.8 points, 10.8 rebounds, and 8.8 assists. The Trail Blazers won the first two games by a total of 7 points before Minnesota won the third game 94–87 on its home court. Portland closed out the series with an 85–77 victory.

THE LOSS OF A FRIEND

Minnesota's final game of the season came on May 2. Eighteen days later, Sealy died in an auto accident while coming home from Garnett's birthday party.

Malik Sealy's jersey is retired and raised to the ceiling of the Target Center before the Timberwolves' home opener November 4, 2000.

The loss of Sealy left a huge void in Garnett's life. He didn't speak to the media for weeks about the death of his friend, idol, mentor, and teammate. When he finally did have something to say, he went to the Internet and posted his thoughts on his Web site.

"(It's) messed up that my man's gone, but I know he's gone to a better place and that's what's keeping me so strong," Garnett wrote. "I think of the good times both on and off the court. I feel so special because my dream of not only playing in the NBA came true, but to play with a guy who I grew up trying to be like, my life is so complete, I only wish ya'll were me and that ya'll could have been around him like I was blessed to be.

"I thank everybody for showing their love, not only for me but for my dogg, you know, it means a lot. My dogg's in a better place now and I feel better knowing that he's there. . . . Rest in peace, Lik."[2]

Garnett still does not like to talk about Sealy, but he did give a hint as to what Sealy meant to him.

"There are two things that I don't really like to talk about," Garnett said a couple of years after Sealy's death. "My private life and Malik. The issue with Malik is sensitive.

"Malik, man, got me to understand life outside of basketball (and at the same time) really enjoy the NBA. Um . . . the life we live, taking advantage of seeing every place . . . I look at my relationship with Malik, and how it happened, and all I ever come up with, is that it was meant."[3]

GIVING BACK

Since becoming a multimillionaire with his first NBA contract as a rookie, Garnett has always tried to give back to the community. One of his favorite charities is The Boys and Girls Club. When he was young, Garnett said he "grew up" in a Boys and Girls Club. The organization helped him grow into a young man and learn how to interact with other kids.

OLYMPICS OFFERS SOLACE

With the 2000 Summer Olympics on the horizon, Garnett had to turn his attention to Team USA and the upcoming competition. The team gathered in Hawaii for some workouts before heading to Asia, where the squad played a series of warm-up games in Japan.

In typical fashion, Garnett became a fan favorite thanks to his outgoing personality. Making his third trip to Japan, Garnett conducted a clinic with some of the country's top teenagers. While talking to the players, Garnett wanted to see them dunk the ball.

At first, no one volunteered. Eventually, one player stepped forward. Taking the ball, he galloped toward the basket, leapt into the air, and clanged the ball off the rim. Garnett quickly took the teenager under his wing and gave him some pointers.

"The kid was just being a little bit too cool," Garnett said of the teen's first attempt. "He knew he could dunk. But there's a certain way you've got to dunk. I had to really take him back to the foundations of dunking."[4]

TOO INTENSE?

Garnett has always been known as one of the most intense and competitive players on the basketball court. Garnett has said that his worst habit on the court is getting too upset with himself. He says he always tries to push and motivate himself, but that he sometimes gets too angry at himself on the court.

Garnett remembers what it was like to learn to dunk the ball. His first dunk came when he was fourteen years old.

"The thing about dunking that I could never understand was the timing," Garnett said. "I could jump, but I just couldn't get my timing right."[5]

After arriving in Sydney, Garnett did his best to spread good cheer. He formed friendships with nearly everyone he met at the Olympic Village.

On the court, Team USA cruised into the medal round before running into trouble. After beating Russia by 15 points, the Americans struggled to get past Lithuania. Team USA came away with a heart-stopping 85–83 victory to advance to the gold medal game.

Facing France, Team USA built a comfortable lead before the French rallied to close the game to 76–72 with 4:26 remaining. Garnett came through with a short put-back shot and then banked in a short jumper to increase the lead. Team USA claimed an 85–75 win.

Garnett scored 6 points on 3-of-5 shooting in the gold medal game. He also grabbed 3 rebounds and one assist. For the tournament, he ranked second in scoring on Team USA, with 10.8 points per game. He led the team in rebounds with an average of 9.1.

After receiving his gold medal, Garnett flashed his smile and kissed his medal. Winning the gold did not mean Garnett forgot about Sealy, but it did allow Garnett to enjoy playing basketball.

CHAPTER EIGHT

Establishing Himself On and Off the Court

Garnett was thrilled to have a gold medal in his trophy case, but he was still searching for his first NBA title. That quest has driven him since he entered the NBA in 1995. With Minnesota coming off its first 50-win season, Garnett knew the Timberwolves were destined for great things during the 2000–01 season.

Personally, Garnett was so automatic on the court every night, his greatness was often overlooked. Garnett provided the Timberwolves with whatever they needed—points, rebounds, and game-changing shots.

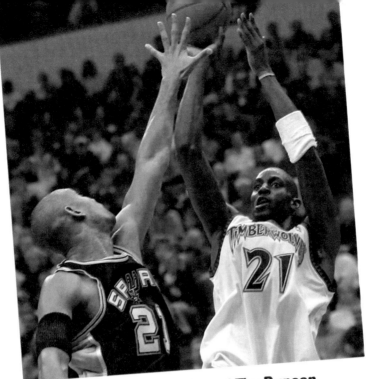

Garnett shoots over the Spurs' Tim Duncan.

By the end of the year, his numbers nearly duplicated his statistics from the year before. He averaged 22 points, 11.4 rebounds, and 5.0 assists. After a slow start as a team, the Timberwolves got going in the second half of the season and finished the year with 47 wins and yet another spot in the playoffs.

Minnesota's first opponent was San Antonio, which bumped the Wolves out of the first round in 1999. History repeated itself in 2001. The Spurs disposed of Minnesota in four games. In the series, Garnett was his usual great self with 21 points, 12 rebounds, and 4.3 assists per game. But that was not enough to slow down Tim Duncan, David Robinson, and the rest of the Spurs.

REACHING OUT TO THE COMMUNITY

Garnett has always been comfortable doing something for others. During the middle of the 2001–02 season, Garnett decided he could offer more and launched 4XL—For Excellence in Leadership—A Kevin Garnett Foundation. The program's goal is to expose minority high school and college students to business environments and help them develop the skills, experience, and relationships that are important in their desired careers.

Garnett holds a limited edition shoe named after him.

The three main components of 4XL are business immersion, leadership development, and technology-based guidance.

"So many young people hope for a bright future but need the roadmap to help them pursue their passions and realize their dreams," Garnett said. "One of my passions is apparel, and I am learning how to be a successful entrepreneur. 4XL provides opportunities for young people to gain exposure, guidance, and access to the business world, and I am excited to learn along with them."[1]

4XL was launched during the All-Star break. Minneapolis-area students Romone Penny and Andrew Porter headed to Philadelphia to learn about the business side of the NBA. Penny and Porter were selected to attend the three-day affair due to their school-related achievements and leadership potential.

Chris Wright, the senior vice president and chief marketing officer of the Timberwolves, was not surprised to learn that Garnett reached out to the community in this way.

"With the leadership position that Kevin is establishing in the NBA, in professional sports overall, and in the mainstream business community, Kevin can teach and achieve so much through his foundation's visionary work in minority communities," Wright said. "Kevin has found yet another unique, high-impact path to give back to the communities in which he lives, works, and plays."[2]

Because of the many endorsement possibilities offered to Garnett, John Rice, the founder and president of Management Leadership for Tomorrow (MLT), believes Garnett is uniquely qualified to reach out to youth in the manner he has. Garnett launched 4XL in partnership with MLT, which helps increase the number of qualified students of color in leading entry-level careers and major graduate business schools as preparation for leadership positions.

"Kevin has the unique ability to influence young people to pursue business careers as well as connect them with executives who can provide expert guidance and open doors to life-changing opportunities," Rice said.[3]

Since 4XL began, the program has benefited hundreds of teenagers and offered them a head start in their careers. 4XL has continued to grow by expanding its reach.

In September 2005, Garnett announced the official opening of the Kevin Garnett 4XL Tech Center at Washburn High School in Minneapolis. The 4XL Foundation teamed with Best Buy, the local nonprofit Achieve!Minneapolis, and the NBA to provide a state-of-the-art learning center that is geared toward helping Washburn students reach their full academic and career potentials.

The center features computers with high-speed Internet access and leading-edge software. Those who have used the center have had access to Garnett's Web-based 4XL program as well.

"The 4XL program provides the online roadmap that all kids need to achieve their goals," Garnett said. "It is critical that we give them the best technology to help create a top-quality learning environment in their schools."[4]

ANOTHER QUICK EXIT

Throughout his career, Garnett always moved around on the offensive end of the court. During the 2001–02 season, he played more like a small forward than a power forward, thanks in large part to a new NBA rule that allowed zone defenses. While some players struggled to adjust to the new rule, Garnett flourished. If smaller opponents guarded Garnett, he could either shoot over them or post them up in the paint. If bigger opponents came out to guard him, Garnett quickly drove right past them and had an easy path to the hoop.

By the end of the season, Garnett had been named Player of the Month four times and finished with more than 19 points, 21 rebounds, and 6 assists per game for the third straight season. Garnett also guided Minnesota to a 50-win season and a berth in the playoffs against Dallas.

Playing Game 1 in Dallas, Garnett was at his best against the Mavericks. Wanting to show critics he and his teammates could finally win a playoff series, Garnett scored 22 points, had 17 rebounds, and

DEVELOP THOSE SKILLS
One of the first things Garnett did after his rookie season was head back to the gym and work on his basketball skills. He believes a person needs to work on the game's fundamentals all of the time, no matter how experienced the player is.

THE GREATEST OF ALL TIME

Garnett has had several idols growing up, but his favorite athlete of all time is Muhammad Ali. He says Ali brought inspiration to a lot of young people and carried himself with dignity and confidence.

handed out 5 assists. But his effort was not good enough. Dallas came away with a 101–94 victory.

After the Game 1 loss, one of Garnett's childhood heroes, Magic Johnson, said Garnett needed to be more aggressive at the end of the game. He was criticizing Garnett for being too much of a team player. Garnett, however, said that has been and always will be his style.

"I don't come in and assess my own stuff," Garnett said. "After a loss, I sit back and think about all the things that I didn't do. I'm not really thinking about it from an individual standpoint, I'm just thinking as a whole what we have to do."[5]

While Garnett understands basketball is a team sport, he also knows the Timberwolves do well when he does well. Garnett led the team with 31 points, 18 rebounds, and 4 assists in Game 2. Szczerbiak and Chauncey Billups each contributed 25 points. Still, that was not good enough, with Dallas prevailing 122–100 to take a 2–0 lead in the series.

"It's reality and we've got to deal with it," Garnett said. "We've got to go home and it's a must that we get these two, starting with this one Sunday."[6]

Despite playing in front of a boisterous home crowd, the Timberwolves were unable to get a win on their own court to extend the series. Garnett posted his usual big numbers and ended the three-game series averaging 24 points, 18.7 rebounds, and 5 assists. But he was not good enough to end a streak of six straight first-round exits, tying a record set by Portland from 1993 to 1998.

After the game, Garnett showed some frustration. The key to winning, he said, was to keep the same team together for more than a year or two. It was a rare outburst for Garnett.

"If you look at all of the other teams in the playoffs, their core has been there consistently," Garnett said. "Every year it seems to be a different blow to us. Look at a team like Utah—they've been there 30 or 40 years. The only consistency here has been Kevin McHale, Flip, myself, and Sam Mitchell."[7]

DID YOU KNOW?
Always available to the media before and after games, Garnett has been voted to the All-Interview Team four times during his career.

A WORD OF ADVICE
Playing in the NBA, Garnett knows the league is a business, making it hard to enjoy going to the arena all the time. But Garnett's advice to young boys and girls is for them to enjoy the game of basketball first and foremost and not let anything take away from the fun of the game.

CHAPTER NINE

Reaching New Heights

Losing to Dallas in the playoffs left Garnett emotionally drained. Critics were growing louder in their claims that Garnett could not win when it mattered most. Garnett had two options. He could give up on his team and demand a trade as so many veterans in sports have done throughout the years, or he could try to improve his game even more.

Garnett could not quit. That had never been an option for him in the past, and it was not an option now. Garnett decided that if Minnesota was going to win in the postseason, he was going to be the driving force behind that success.

Each day he worked tirelessly in the gym to improve his game, shooting jumper after jumper and

Garnett and some teammates watch the end of a game against the Toronto Raptors from the bench on November 1, 2003.

working on his dribbling skills. Garnett did not stop there. He worked with a nutritionist to improve his diet. He spent time with a personal trainer to improve his stamina and make him stronger and leaner for the next season.

Determined to lead the franchise to postseason glory, "The Big Ticket," as Garnett was often referred to now, elevated his game to a level he had not reached before. After putting up the numbers he did in the last three seasons, that seemed hard to do. Around the league, he was already considered one of the best players in the game.

In a preseason survey of NBA general managers by NBA.com, Garnett was voted the most versatile defender in the league, receiving 23.1 percent of the vote. Tracy McGrady and Ben Wallace tied for second with 11.5 percent of the vote. In a nod toward Garnett's amazing versatility on the court, he was voted second-best small forward in the league, behind Tracy McGrady, and the second-best power forward, behind Tim Duncan. He also finished fourth in voting for which NBA player has the best athleticism.

KEVIN GARNETT'S ALL-STAR STATISTICS

YEAR	MINUTES	POINTS	REBOUNDS	BLOCKS	ASSISTS	STEALS
1997	18	6	9	1	1	0
1998	21	12	4	1	2	2
1999	35	24	10	1	5	1
2001	27	14	4	3	4	1
2002	24	14	12	0	2	2
2003	41	37	9	1	3	5
2004	29	12	7	1	6	2
2005	16	10	3	0	2	0
2006	16	2	9	0	4	1

From the start of the season, Garnett looked like a man who had something to prove. If it was a clutch situation, Garnett was demanding the ball from teammates. More often than not, he came through, too. Garnett was putting up career numbers, and the Timberwolves were winning at a record pace.

ON AN MVP PACE

On both ends of the court, Garnett was establishing himself as a dominant force in the league. Some players were scoring more points, but they were not matching Garnett's rebounding ability, both offensively and defensively. Players his size were not in the same league when it came to passing the ball. He recorded double-digit assists three times. Against the best players in the league at the 2003 All-Star Game, Garnett earned the MVP award after scoring 37 points, grabbing 9 rebounds, and coming away with 5 steals.

As Minnesota battled for playoff seeding down the stretch, Garnett was at his best. He finished April averaging 21 points, 15 rebounds, 8 assists, and 2 blocks per game. Against Portland, he had 16 points, 14 rebounds, and 12 assists, collecting his league-leading sixth triple-double. Garnett was named Player of the Month for April.

After the game against Portland, Garnett was more concerned with where the team stood in the standings, not where he stood with voters for the MVP award.

Garnett and Kendall Gill react as their team takes the lead during overtime of Game 3 in a playoff series in 2003.

"I told the guys before the game that this is the first game of the playoffs," Garnett said. "If we lose this game, then we're pretty much out of the race for the fourth seed."[1]

Thanks in large part to Garnett, Minnesota went 5–2 in April to finish the season with a franchise-record 51 wins. More important, the team had home-court advantage in the playoffs for the first time.

The Wolves faced the Los Angeles Lakers in the first round. The two teams split the first two games before Minnesota claimed Game 3 with a 114–110 overtime win. More impressive was the fact the Wolves won the game with Garnett sitting on the bench for most of the overtime period. After scoring 33 points and grabbing 14 rebounds, Garnett fouled out only 12 seconds into the overtime period on a questionable call.

"It was miserable, knowing I couldn't come out there and help my team," Garnett said. "I thought of other ways to help out, motivate, help the guys get over the edge.

"I was going to be a T-Wolves cheerleader without the skirt and pom-poms."[2]

Troy Hudson, who had 27 points, said the encouraging words Garnett uttered to his teammates while heading to the bench were vital.

"When you have a superstar go out of the game, it usually takes the breath out of a team," Hudson said. "Our guys just stepped up. He just told us, 'Those five guys who are out there, you have to believe in yourselves.'"[3]

The thrilling overtime victory, however, would be the last in the series for Minnesota. As was the case in 1997, 1998, 1999, 2000, 2001, and 2002, the Timberwolves were bounced from the playoffs in the first round. The Lakers won the series 4–2. In Game 6,

Garnett had his sixth straight double-double with 18 points and 12 rebounds. He finished the series averaging 27 points and 15.7 rebounds. But it was not enough—again.

"I am disappointed," Garnett said. "We did a lot of good things in this series. I think that we tested them a little bit. We sort of got under their skin a little bit. But they turned it up when they had to."[4]

Making matters worse for Garnett was the fact he fell short of winning the MVP award. Garnett set career highs in points scored (23.0), rebounds (13.5), and assists (6.0) and joined Larry Bird and Wilt Chamberlain as the only players in NBA history to average 20 points, 10 rebounds, and 5 assists for the fourth year in a row. But in a close vote, Tim Duncan of San Antonio was named the MVP for the second consecutive year.

FINALLY BREAKING THROUGH

Minnesota was close to breaking its first-round curse. All that was needed was some experienced depth to complement Garnett. During the off-season, McHale was able to bring in point guard Sam Cassell, a veteran who had won two NBA titles as a member of the Houston Rockets in 1994 and 1995. Latrell Sprewell was also brought in, as well as center Michael Olowokandi and reserves Fred Hoiberg and Mark Madsen.

> **DID YOU KNOW?**
>
> Garnett married long-time girlfriend Brandi Padilla in the summer of 2004 during a private ceremony in California. The wedding was the reason he did not take part in the Summer Olympic Games. Padilla is the sister-in-law of Jimmy Jam Harris, one of Garnett's close friends.

How confident was Garnett in McHale's moves during the off-season? Believing the team was ready for greatness, he signed a five-year contract extension for $100 million.

"I had the solid pieces around me that I felt I could go forward, and that's my loyalty," said Garnett about why he signed the extension. "That's what I do. I'm not a person to jump up and down, I'm not a guy to go market to market, you know, that's not me. Once I saw them step up and obtain Latrell and Sam and put some really good additions around me, Ervin Johnson and a whole bunch of other pieces, it looked good, and I looked at it and I was like, well, this is it."[5]

Cassell and Sprewell were a perfect fit in Minnesota. They were able to take the scoring load off Garnett. At the same time, they knew Garnett was the focal point on offense. As a team, the Timberwolves proved to be one of the best clubs in the league.

As the season progressed, Garnett looked more and more like an MVP candidate. He started the season with a bang, scoring 25 points and grabbing 21 rebounds against Milwaukee. He never looked back.

After a sluggish start through November, Minnesota hit its stride. With Garnett leading the way, the Timberwolves won 11 of 13 games in December, 12 of 15 games in January, and 11 of 15 games in February to build a 43–17 record. By the end of the season, Minnesota had won a franchise-record and Western Conference-best 58 games. The Wolves entered the playoffs as the top seed.

In December, Garnett put up outrageous numbers. In a contest against Sacramento, Garnett was a monster on the boards, finishing with a franchise-record 25 rebounds. With the game on the line against the Kings, Garnett drained 2 three-pointers in the final 30 seconds to send the contest into overtime. Facing the Clippers a couple of days later, Garnett called for the ball with the game on the line. With time ticking away, he drained the game-winning shot as the buzzer sounded.

DID YOU KNOW?

When Garnett was named the NBA's Most Valuable Player in 2004, it was the first league MVP winner for a Minnesota player in the NBA, NFL, NHL, or Major League Baseball since 1977, when Rod Carew won the American League MVP award for the Twins.

Individually, Garnett had his best season. He scored a career-high 24.2 points per game and grabbed a career-high and league-leading 13.9 rebounds per game while dishing out 5.7 assists per contest. When the voting for the league MVP was announced, Garnett won in a landslide, garnering 120 of the 123

GIVING THANKS

In November, Garnett has participated in the Wolves Give Thanks event, in which he and others served Thanksgiving dinner and took part in activities with family members of military personnel. He has also gone shopping with ten foster children during the Wolves Season of Giving in December. His work in the community earned him the NBA Community Assist Award for the month of November in 2005.

first-place votes. Garnett was overjoyed with the MVP award. But, as usual, he thought of his teammates first when asked about how it felt to be the MVP winner.

"I wouldn't be nothing without those knuckleheads, believe me," Garnett said. "It's a team game, and I've always kept that perspective."[6]

Shaquille O'Neal was happy to see Garnett nab the award.

"He's definitely deserving of it," said O'Neal. "He waited his turn. A lot of people thought he should've won it last year."[7]

Garnett had reached the highest level on an individual stage. The question was whether the Timberwolves would finally reach the highest level on a team stage.

CHAPTER TEN

A Leader and a Giver

Everyone in Minneapolis was yelling and screaming, releasing the type of cheer never heard by Timberwolves fans. On the court, the celebration was just as happy and intense. In the middle of the chaotic scene was Kevin Garnett.

Seven years of playoff failure and the ever-growing criticism about Garnett's ability to lead his team to victory in the playoffs were gone. Thanks to Garnett and his outstanding play in the first round of the 2004 playoffs, the Timberwolves defeated Denver three games to one.

"I am not a quitter," Garnett said after the game. "I won't quit on nothing, especially when it is something like not getting out of the first round. It is not in me to quit.

KEVIN GARNETT'S POSTSEASON STATISTICS

YEAR	MINUTES	POINTS	REBOUNDS	BLOCKS	ASSISTS	STEALS
1997	3	17.3	28	3	11	4
1998	5	15.8	48	12	20	4
1999	4	21.8	48	8	15	7
2000	4	18.8	43	3	35	5
2001	4	21.0	48	6	17	4
2002	3	24.0	56	5	15	5
2003	6	27.0	94	10	31	10
2004	18	24.3	263	41	92	24

"I am very excited. I am not going to downplay it. I am eager to see what is on the other side."[1]

Against the Nuggets, Minnesota received big games from either Cassell or Sprewell, but Garnett delivered throughout the series, averaging 25.8 points, 14.8 rebounds, 7 assists, and 2 blocked shots. In the second game of the series, Sprewell hit 7 three-pointers and finished with 31 points.

Sprewell took advantage of Denver's desire to try to slow down Garnett. Double-teamed by two Denver defenders, Garnett whipped a pass to Sprewell, who was standing behind the three-point line. Launching a wide-open shot, Sprewell sank the trey. That same scene played out again and again.

By the end of the night, Garnett had 10 assists to go along with 20 points and 22 rebounds. He also added 3 blocked shots and was a force on defense throughout the night. It was the third career triple-double for Garnett. After the game, however, Garnett was upset with his performance because he made only 9 of his 27 shots from the floor.

"I played like garbage," said Garnett, who has always been his toughest critic. "But this is not a time to leave bullets in the gun. I'm going to still come out shooting. But tonight I tried to do different things, to get my teammates involved."[2]

Garnett works the ball inside for a shot against the Denver Nuggets on April 24, 2004.

While clinching the fifth game of the series, Garnett put in what was becoming a typical game for him. Garnett's dunking and jump shooting skills led to 28 points. His jumping ability and perfect timing allowed him to snag 7 rebounds. Whenever Denver was able to double him, his uncanny ability and floor vision led to 8 assists.

Whatever Minnesota needed from him, Garnett was there to deliver. The Nuggets closed to within six points, 72–66, late in the third quarter. Garnett simply took over from there. After sinking two free throws to end the quarter, he scored 8 points in the first four minutes of the fourth quarter to give Minnesota a 14-point lead. Garnett capped his run with a fadeaway jumper over two defenders and brought the crowd to its feet.

"I have been in a lot of series and I have been in that position before and I knew we needed a lift," Garnett said. "I called all the sets. I told the team that I am going to put it on my back. I have learned from experience.

"I just told everybody, 'Bump all this and play off me.'"[3]

Nuggets coach Jeff Bzdelick summed up Garnett's hard-working attitude and desire to do whatever it takes to win.

"He is a superstar that has a blue-collar attitude, and that is great," Bzdelick said.[4]

KINGS UP NEXT

The second round featured a matchup against Sacramento. In seven tough games during the series, Minnesota escaped to advance to the conference finals.

Playing in his first Game 7, the pressure was on Garnett to perform and show he was a deserving MVP. Garnett was masterful. He scored 32 points, hauled down 21 rebounds, and swatted away 5 shots. His effort allowed the Wolves to celebrate an 83–80 victory against the Kings and celebrate Garnett's twenty-eighth birthday in style.

Garnett was a one-man show in the fourth quarter. He started with a blocked shot, his third of the game, and dominated the contest for the last nine minutes. Grabbing a defensive rebound, Garnett hustled down the court and got in position near the paint. Receiving a pass from Szczerbiak, Garnett nailed a turnaround jumper to give the Wolves a 66–62 lead with 8:50 remaining. The jumper was the start of a string of 13 straight points scored by Garnett.

Following the turnaround jumper was a driving layup with 7:35 remaining. Then came a hook shot in the lane 28 seconds later. Fouled on the shot, Garnett sank the free throw. Completing the highlight reel streak was a fast break, a thunderous dunk, and a jump shot to give Minnesota a 7-point lead with 3:39 remaining.

"I felt like I had to be aggressive," Garnett said. "I felt like I had to be the example to everybody. I

Peja Stojakovic fouls Garnett in the final minutes of Game 7 of the 2004 NBA Western Conference semifinal series.

didn't want to come out here and then later on be sitting by myself or driving home and wondering if I could've done more."[5]

"In this situation—with the impact of the game—he's maybe never been better," Minnesota coach Flip Saunders said.[6]

Garnett's heroics were not just on the offensive end. Near the end of the game, Garnett came up with his fourth steal and his fifth block to keep the Kings from scoring down the stretch.

"There was a ton of pressure on him, but he had an amazing calm about him," Saunders said. "He didn't even have to work tonight. He was in such a flow offensively and defensively."[7]

TITLE DREAMS COME TO AN END

Garnett's hopes of winning an NBA title to cap his MVP season came to an end in the Western Conference Finals. The Lakers, who knocked the Timberwolves out of the playoffs in 2003, did so again by taking the series in six games.

Against Los Angeles, Garnett had a double-double in each game and nearly had a triple-double in Game 4, but his 23.7 points, 13.5 rebounds, and 4.5 assists per contest were not enough. A slow start in Game 6—and a sluggish fourth quarter—buried the Wolves. The fact the team was playing without Cassell, who was out with a sore hip and back, did not help matters.

"The fact that we did not have our general out there with us sure took us off a little bit," Garnett said. "Guys were asked to do things they don't normally do. We all took up the responsibility and ran with it. We still had a chance to win."[8]

After such a successful season, Minnesota had high hopes entering the 2004–05 season. But the Timberwolves were never able to find their rhythm and ended up with a 44–38 record. They missed the playoffs for the first time since Garnett's rookie season.

Garnett and Devean George go after a rebound in Game 2 of
the NBA Western Conference Finals on May 23, 2004.

Garnett nearly duplicated his numbers from the
season before, averaging 22.2 points, 13.5 rebounds,
and 5.7 assists. He led the league in rebounding for the
second consecutive year. But Cassell missed 23 games,
and his absence was too much to overcome.

It only got worse for Minnesota in 2005–06. With
both Cassell and Sprewell no longer with the club, the

Timberwolves missed the postseason and finished 33–49, the team's first losing season since 1996–97. Garnett led the league in rebounding once again, pulling down 12.7 per game, but that was little comfort to him due to the team's struggles.

GARNETT COMES UP BIG

Before the start of the 2005–06 season, Hurricane Katrina devastated the Gulf Coast of the United States. Making landfall on August 29, 2005, just east of New

RECOGNIZED FOR HIS CHARITABLE WORK

Kevin Garnett has given both time and money to those in need throughout his career without expecting anything in return. His generosity was recognized in the summer of 2006 when he was named the recipient of the J. Walter Kennedy Citizenship Award, presented annually by the Professional Basketball Writers Association (PBWA). The Kennedy Citizenship Award is named for the league's second commissioner and is the oldest citizenship and community service award in the NBA.

Garnett said he was honored to receive the award and is happy he is in a position to help make a difference. Garnett often does a lot of charitable work in private, but his $1.2 million donation to aid the Hurricane Katrina relief effort and the work of his 4XL Foundation have been hard to keep quiet.

The PBWA represents writers for newspapers, magazines, and Internet services who cover the NBA on a regular basis. Members nominate players for the award. Then, a vote is taken by the membership of approximately 150.

Orleans, the storm ravaged the coasts of Louisiana, Mississippi, and Alabama. Estimated damage from the storm was $75 billion, making Katrina the costliest hurricane in the country's history.

DID YOU KNOW?

Garnett grew up with two sisters, Sonya and Ashley, but he also has four half brothers. O'Lewis McCullough, Garnett's father, has four other children, Christopher, O'Lewis Jr., Isaac, and Kenneth.

More than 1,800 people died in the storm. Thousands were left homeless. Garnett knew he had to do something for those families that were now homeless and had scattered throughout the country in an effort to find shelter. Garnett donated $1.2 million to build homes for victims in the New Orleans area and throughout the Gulf Coast region. His donation will build one house a month for the next two years.

"I knew I wanted to do something," Garnett said. "But I didn't know in detail what I wanted to do."[9]

Garnett teamed up with Oprah Winfrey's Angel Network charity foundation for the project. He chose her foundation because 100 percent of his donation will go toward the victims.

"I'm from the South, and I know how hard the South is," Garnett said. "A lot of things that go on up North, there's a lot more opportunity.

DID YOU KNOW?

Garnett scored a career-high 47 points against the Phoenix Suns on January 4, 2005. He made 19 of his 28 shots and 9 of his 11 free throws. In addition, he grabbed 17 rebounds, had 4 assists, and blocked 2 shots.

In the South, there's not as much opportunity and I know it's going to be a dramatic and drastic transition to turn that city around.

"I'm not the one for a lot of publicity, I'm not one to put myself out there with what I do, but in this case, I hope that it motivates others to give."[10]

Though Garnett does not like to boast about his good works, others have noticed. In October 2006, he earned the J. Walter Kennedy Citizenship award, which is presented by the Professional Basketball Writers Association.

PURSUIT OF TITLE CONTINUES

After eleven seasons in the NBA, Garnett has accomplished nearly everything one individual can. However, the team has failed to win a title with Garnett on the floor and took a step backward in 2004–05. Minnesota then shed Cassell and Sprewell and surrounded Garnett with the talented but inexperienced Marko Jaric and rookie Rashad McCants. The moves left Garnett a little frustrated before the start of the 2005–06 campaign.

"Whether you put faith in them or not, they do what they want to do," he said during the preseason when asked about the team's off-season moves. "It's not my team. [Owner] Glen Taylor and Kevin [McHale] put together a plan and then, for whatever reason, I guess, try to enforce it. I don't think I'm the person to ask about that. Ask them."[11]

After uttering those words, Garnett was in the center of trade rumors throughout the 2005–06 season and into the off-season. But the rumors were just that—rumors.

"We're not going to trade Kevin Garnett," said McHale. "Teams that would call up (to trade for Garnett) have nothing I would trade him for anyway.

"Kevin wants to win. Kevin is very competitive. The last conversation we had—about a week ago, he came in for a couple of hours and we talked—he said he understands where we're at with this team and how, hopefully, a piece or two could make a real difference."[12]

Winning is all that has ever mattered to Garnett. Everything he has done on the court on an individual level has been spectacular. However, Garnett would trade all of that for a title.

"I've always told my teammates, 'If you don't think we're going to win it, if you're not in here to lay it down on the line and push for the world championship, then leave. Because you're wasting your time, you're wasting our time.' We're here to win."[13]

> **DID YOU KNOW?**
>
> On January 18, 2006, Garnett grabbed the 9,000th regular season rebound of his career in a game against the Boston Celtics. He became only the sixth player in NBA history to have at least 16,000 points, 9,000 rebounds, and 3,500 assists. Only Wilt Chamberlain, Elgin Baylor, Kareem Abdul-Jabbar, Charles Barkley, and Karl Malone have also accomplished the feat.

CAREER STATISTICS

YEAR	GAMES	AVERAGE	REBOUNDS
1995–96	80	10.4	501
1996–97	77	17.0	618
1997–98	82	18.5	786
1999	47	20.8	489
1999–2000	81	22.9	956
2000–01	81	22.0	921
2001–02	81	21.2	981
2002–03	82	23.0	1102
2003–04	82	24.2	1139
2004–05	82	22.2	1108
2005–06	76	21.8	966
Totals	851	20.4	9,567

BLOCKS	ASSISTS	STEALS
131	145	86
163	236	105
150	348	139
83	202	78
126	401	120
145	401	111
126	422	96
129	495	113
178	409	120
112	466	121
107	308	104
1,450	3,833	1,193

CAREER ACHIEVEMENTS

- Named the NBA's MVP in 2004

- Only player in NBA history to average 20 points, 10 rebounds, and 5 assists in 6 straight seasons

- Only player in NBA history to reach at least 17,000 points, 9,500 rebounds, 3,800 assists, 1,190 steals, and 1,450 blocks in his playing career

- Named to the All-Star team nine straight seasons (no game held in 1999)

- Named All-NBA First Team, Second Team, or Third Team seven times during his career

- Named to the All-Rookie Second Team in 1996

- Earned All-Defensive First Team honors six times and Second Team honors once

- Named the MVP of the 2003 All-Star Game

- Earned the J. Walter Kennedy Citizenship Award in 2006

- Led NBA in rebounding in 2003–04, 2004–05, and 2005–06

- First NBA player to receive four Player of the Month honors in one season

- Earned Player of the Month honors eight times and Player of the Week honors twelve times

- Recorded fourteen regular season triple-doubles and two postseason triple-doubles

CHAPTER NOTES

CHAPTER 1. BLAZING A TRAIL

1. "Garnett leads West to win in McDonald's game," *Kentucky Kernel*, April 3, 1995, <http://www.kernel.uky.edu/1995/spring/040395/040332.html> (May 19, 2006).

2. "High school star Kevin Garnett makes himself eligible for NBA Draft," *Jet*, May 29, 1995, <http://www.findarticles.com/p/articles/mi_m1355/is_n3_v88/ai_17018371> (May 18, 2006).

3. Ibid.

4. Brett Ballantini, "'The Kid' grows up: leading his best Minnesota team yet, Kevin Garnett has expanded his game and is pushing the Timberwolves to dizzying heights," *Basketball Digest*, March, 2002, <http://www.findarticles.com/p/articles/mi_m0FCJ/is_5_29/ai_83446818/pg_2> (May 17, 2006).

5. Michael Wilbon, "Prep Star Garnett is NBA's Fool Gold," *Washington Post*, May 28, 1995, <http://sports-law.blogspot.com/2005/10/kevin-garnett-10-years-and-30000.html> (May 19, 2006).

6. Jay Mariotti, "Does Garnett Have Any Idea of What He is Getting Into?," *Chicago Sun-Times*, June 20, 1995, <http://sports-law.blogspot.com/2005/10/kevin-garnett-10-years-and-30000.html> (May 19, 2006).

7. Brad Weinstein, "Preps to Pros: Record numbers are entering NBA Draft," SFGate.com, May 13, 2001, <http://sfgate.com/cgi-bin/article.cgi?file=/chronicle/archive/2001/05/13/SP149155.DTL> (May 10, 2006).

8. Ibid.

9. Bob Carter, " 'Da Kid' progressed quickly," ESPN.com, n.d., <http://espn.go.com/classic/biography/s/Garnett_Kevin.html> (May 10, 2006).

10. Ibid.

11. Joe Gioia, "The $126 million man," Salon.com, February 12, 2000, <http://archive.salon.com/people/feature/2000/02/12/garnett/index1.html> (May 18, 2006).

CHAPTER 2. GROWING UP IN SOUTH CAROLINA

1. Ellen Tomson, "Kevin Garnett: Passion Play," TwinCities.com, November 30, 1997, <http://extra.twincities.com/garnett/> (May 19, 2006).

2. Joe Gioia, "The $126 million man," Salon.com, February 12, 2000, <http://archive.salon.com/people/feature/2000/02/12/garnett/index1.html> (May 18, 2006).

3. Robert "Scoop" Jackson, "The Man," *Hoop Magazine,* n.d. <http://www.nba.com/features/hoop_kg_040219.html> (May 16, 2006).

4. Ellen Tomson, "Kevin Garnett: Passion Play," TwinCities.com, November 30, 1997, <http://extra.twincities.com/garnett/> (May 19, 2006).

5. Bob Carter, " 'Da Kid' progressed quickly," ESPN.com, n.d., <http://espn.go.com/classic/biography/s/Garnett_Kevin.html> (May 10, 2006).

6. Ellen Tomson, "Kevin Garnett: Passion Play," TwinCities.com, November 30, 1997, <http://extra.twincities.com/garnett/> (May 19, 2006).

7. Ibid.

8. Joe Gioia, "The $126 million man," Salon.com, February 12, 2000, <http://archive.salon.com/people/feature/2000/02/12/garnett/index1.html> (May 18, 2006).

9. Ibid.

10. Bob Carter, " 'Da Kid' progressed quickly," ESPN.com, n.d., <http://espn.go.com/classic/biography/s/Garnett_Kevin.html> (May 10, 2006).

11. Ellen Tomson, "Kevin Garnett: Passion Play," TwinCities.com, November 30, 1997, <http://extra.twincities.com/garnett/> (May 19, 2006).

CHAPTER 3. LEAVING FOR CHICAGO

1. Ellen Tomson, "Kevin Garnett: Passion Play," TwinCities.com, November 30, 1997, <http://extra.twincities.com/garnett/> (May 19, 2006).

2. Frank Clancy, "The kid's all right," *The Sporting News,* March 4, 1996, <http://www.highbeam.com/library/docfree/asp?DOCID=1G1:18064184&ctrlInfo=Round20%3Amode20e%3AdocG%3Aresults&ao> (May 20, 2006).

3. Ibid.

4. Ellen Tomson, "Kevin Garnett: Passion Play," TwinCities.com, November 30, 1997, <http://extra.twincities.com/garnett/> (May 19, 2006).

5. Ibid.

6. Frank Clancy, "The kid's all right," *The Sporting News,* March 4, 1996, <http://www.highbeam.com/library/docfree/asp?DOCID=1G1:18064184&ctrlInfo=Round20%3Amode20e%3AdocG%3Aresults&ao> (May 20, 2006).

7. Ellen Tomson, "Kevin Garnett: Passion Play," TwinCities.com, November 30, 1997, <http://extra.twincities.com/garnett/> (May 19, 2006).

8. David Nakamura, "Joe Goes West as Warriors Make Smith No.1 Pick," *Washington Post,* June 29, 1995, <http://www.washingtonpost.com/wp-srv/sports/longterm/memories/1995/95nba3.htm> (May 20, 2006).

CHAPTER 4. ADJUSTING TO THE NBA

1. Frank Clancy, "The kid's all right," *The Sporting News,* March 4, 1996, <http://www.highbeam.com/library/docfree/asp?DOCID=1G1:18064184&ctrlInfo=Round20%3Amode20e%3AdocG%3Aresults&ao> (May 20, 2006).

2. Rachel Bachman, "Kevin the Kid," *Timberwolves Tonight*, November 22, 1995, <http://aol.nba.com/timberwolves/features/garnett_951122.html> (May 21, 2006).

3. Frank Clancy, "The kid's all right," *The Sporting News*, March 4, 1996, <http://www.highbeam.com/library/docfree/asp?DOCID=1G1:18064184&ctrl Info=Round20%3Amode20e%3AdocG%3Aresults&ao>(May 20, 2006).

4. Rachel Bachman, "Kevin the Kid," *Timberwolves Tonight*, November 22, 1995, <http://aol.nba.com/timberwolves/features/garnett_951122.html> (May 21, 2006).

5. Frank Clancy, "The kid's all right," *The Sporting News*, March 4, 1996, <http://www.highbeam.com/library/docfree/asp?DOCID=1G1:18064184&ctrl Info=Round20%3Amode20e%3AdocG%3Aresults&ao> (May 20, 2006).

6. Rachel Bachman, "Kevin the Kid," *Timberwolves Tonight*, November 22, 1995, <http://aol.nba.com/timberwolves/features/garnett_951122.html> (May 21, 2006).

7. Frank Clancy, "The kid's all right," *The Sporting News*, March 4, 1996, <http://www.highbeam.com/library/docfree/asp?DOCID=1G1:18064184&ctrl Info=Round20%3Amode20e%3AdocG%3Aresults&ao> (May 20, 2006).

8. Ibid.

9. Joe Gioia, "The $126 million man," Salon.com, February 12, 2000, <http://archive.salon.com/people/feature/2000/02/12/garnett/index1.html> (May 18, 2006).

10. Frank Clancy, "The kid's all right," *The Sporting News*, March 4, 1996, <http://www.highbeam.com/library/docfree/asp?DOCID=1G1:18064184&ctrl Info=Round20%3Amode20e%3AdocG%3Aresults&ao> (May 20, 2006).

CHAPTER 5. LEADING THE WOLVES TO THE POSTSEASON

1. Rachel Bachman, "Kevin the Kid," *Timberwolves Tonight*, November 22, 1995, <http://aol.nba.com/timberwolves/features/garnett_951122.html> (May 21, 2006).

2. Shaun Powell, "The Bulls are a lock, and other random thoughts," *The Sporting News*, February 10, 1997, <http://www.findarticles.com/p/articles/mi_m1208/is_n6_v221/ai_19105587> (May 22, 2006).

3. Bob Carter, " 'Da Kid' progressed quickly," ESPN.com, n.d., <http://espn.go.com/classic/biography/s/Garnett_Kevin.html> (May 10, 2006).

CHAPTER 6. GARNETT MAKES HISTORY AGAIN

1. "Kevin Garnett Timeline," *Garnett Tribute*, October 1, 1997, <http://www.geocities.com/garnetttribute/timeline.html> (May 20, 2006).

2. Ibid.

3. Tim Kurkjian, "Pro Basketball '97: Minnesota Timberwolves scouting report," *Sports Illustrated*, n.d., <http://sportsillustrated.cnn.com/basketball/nba/events/1997/nbapreview/timberwolves.html> (May 25, 2006).

4. Britt Robson, "Great Expectations," *CityPages*.com, October 15, 1997, <http://citypages.com/databank/18/880/article1965.asp> (May 23, 2006).

5. "Timberwolves vs. Sonics: Game Recap," *USAToday*.com, April 24, 1998, <http://www.usatoday.com/sports/scores98/98116/98116408.htm> (May 23, 2006).

6. "Sonics vs. Timberwolves: Game Recap," *USAToday*.com, April 28, 1998, <http://www.usatoday.com/sports/scores98/98118/98118393.htm> (May 23, 2006).

7. Ibid.

8. "Timberwolves must wait to see what future holds," *USAToday*.com, n.d., <http://www.usatoday.com/sports/basketba/98play/play061.htm> (May 23, 2006).

CHAPTER 7. PICKING UP THE PIECES

1. Mike Monroe, "Olympics is a tough sell for Team USA," *San Antonio Express-News*, January 8, 2006, <http://www.mysanantonio.com/sports/columnists/mmonroe/stories/MYSA010806.8C.COL.BKNmonroe.olympics.2dc53f3.html> (May 25, 2006).

2. "Garnett goes to the 'Net about Sealy's death," *Coastal Bend Health*, May 24, 2000, <http://www.coastalbendhealth.com/2000/may/24/today/sports_n/718.html> (May 23, 2006).

3. Robert "Scoop" Jackson, "The Man," *Hoop Magazine*, n.d. <http://www.nba.com/features/hoop_kg_040219.html> (May 16, 2006).

4. "Americans were successful on and off the court," ESPN.com, September 19, 2000, <http://espn.go.com/oly/summer00/basketball/s/2000/0907/728521.html> (May 21, 2006).

5. Ibid.

CHAPTER 8. ESTABLISHING HIMSELF ON AND OFF THE COURT

1. "Kevin Garnett Launches 4XL in Partnership with MLT," ML4T.org, February 18, 2002, <http://www.ml4t.org/v2/4xl_news1.html> (May 19, 2006).

2. Ibid.

3. Ibid.

4. "NBA superstar donates technology center to support academic achievement, career preparation for Washburn students," 4XL.com, September 29, 2005, <http://4xl.monster.com/4xl_news8.asp> (May 19, 2006).

5. "Recap: Dallas 122, Minnesota 110," SI.com, April 25, 2002, <http://sportsillustrated.cnn.com/basketball/nba/recaps/2002/04/24/dal_min/> (May 24, 2006).

6. Ibid.

7. "Recap: Dallas 115, Minnesota 102," SI.com, April 28, 2002, <http://sportsillustrated.cnn.com/basketball/nba/recaps/2002/04/28/min_dal/> (May 24, 2006).

CHAPTER 9. REACHING NEW HEIGHTS

1. "Game Story," databaseBasketball.com, n.d., <http://www.databasebasketball.com/teams/boxscore.htm?yr=2002&b=20030406&tm=Por> (May 22, 2006).

2. "A statement victory: T'wolves rally in OT without Garnett, grab 2-1 series lead," SI.com, April 25, 2003, <http://sportsillustrated.cnn.com/basketball/nba/2003/playoffs/news/2003/04/24/twolves_lakers_ap/> (May 23, 2006).

3. Ibid.

4. "NBA Recap: LA Lakers 101, Minnesota 85," SI.com, May 2, 2003, <http://sportsillustrated.cnn.com/basketball/nba/recaps/2003/05/01/14682_recap.html> (May 23, 2006).

5. "Sunday Conversation: Kevin Garnett," ESPN.com, May 10, 2004, <http://sports.espn.go.com/nba/playoffs2004/news/story?id=1798493> (May 19, 2006).

6. "Minnesota's valuable player: Garnett the MVP," *USAToday*.com, May 3, 2004, <http://www.usatoday.com/sports/basketball/nba/twolves/2004-05-03-garnett-mvp_x.htm> (May 22, 2006).

7. Ibid.

CHAPTER 10. A LEADER AND A GIVER

1. "Wolves End Playoff Drought," NBA.com, April 30, 2004, <http://aol.nba.com/games/20040430/DENMIN/recap.html> (May 22, 2006).

2. "Sprewell Nails Seven Treys, Wolves Romp," NBA.com, April 21, 2004, <http://aol.nba.com/games/20040421/DENMIN/recap.html> (May 22, 2006).

3. "Wolves End Playoff Drought," NBA.com, April 30, 2004, <http://aol.nba.com/games/20040430/DENMIN/recap.html> (May 22, 2006).

4. Ibid.

5. "Garnett Leads Timberwolves to Western Conference Finals," NBA.com, May 19, 2004, <http://aol.nba.com/games/20040519/SACMIN/recap.html> (May 22, 2006).

6. Ibid.

7. Ibid

8. "Rush Rallies Lakers to West Championship," NBA.com, May 31, 2004, <http://aol.nba.com/games/20040531/MINLAL/recap.html> (May 22, 2006).

9. "Garnett donates $1.2 million to Katrina relief fund," ESPN.com, November 11, 2005, <http://sports.espn.go.com/nba/news/story?id=2221292> (May 27, 2006).

10. Ibid.

11. Marty Burns, "Ticketed for elsewhere? Garnett's future rests on Timberwolves' season," SI.com, November 14, 2005, <http://sportsillustrated.cnn.com/2005/writers/marty_burns/11/14/garnett/index.html> (June 2, 2006).

12. "McHale: 'We're Not Going To Trade Kevin Garnett,'" *RealGMbasketball*, June 5, 2006, <http://www.realgm.com/src_wiretap_archives/40793/20060605/mchale_were_not_going_to_trade_kevin_garnett/> (June 8, 2006).

13. Bob Carter, " 'Da Kid' progressed quickly," ESPN.com, n.d., <http://espn.go.com/classic/biography/s/Garnett_Kevin.html> (May 10, 2006).

GLOSSARY

actor—A person who performs in a movie.

assist—A pass that leads to a basket.

charity—The act of giving or an organization that gives to the needy.

contract—A written agreement between a player and a team stating how long the player is expected to be part of the team and how much he will be paid.

director—A person who organizes a movie, instructing the actors, cameramen, etc.

draft—A process in which professional sports teams choose players in order.

field goal—A basket made while the clock is running in basketball; any shot other than a foul shot.

free throw—Also known as a foul shot; attempts given to teams after a foul or technical foul has been called.

Olympics—A sporting competition pitting teams from different countries against one another in multiple sports.

playoffs—A series of games between two teams to eliminate the losing team and send the winning team on to another round until just one team remains as the champion.

post—To establish a position near the basket.

rebound—To gain possession of the basketball after a missed shot.

rookie—A first-year professional.

scholarship—A grant of money to a student for educational purposes; top athletes are offered scholarships by colleges to attend and play sports for their schools.

FOR MORE INFORMATION

FURTHER READING

Molzahn, Arlene Bourgeois. *Kevin Garnett*. Mankato, Minn.: Capstone Press, Inc., 2001.

Torres, John Albert. *Kevin Garnett: "Da Kid."* Minneapolis: Lerner Sports, 1999.

Zuehlke, Jeffrey. *Kevin Garnett*. Minneapolis: First Avenue Editions, 2004.

WEB LINKS

Kevin Garnett's home page:
www.kevingarnett.com

The Timberwolves' team page on NBA.com:
www.NBA.com/timberwolves/

Kevin Garnett's player page on NBA.com:
www.NBA.com/playerfile/kevin_garnett/

Kevin Garnett's 4XL Foundation:
www.ml4t.org/4xl

INDEX

A

Amateur Athletic Union, 25, 26, 27

B

Babcock, Rob, 12–13, 14

Barkley, Charles, 59, 111

Billups, Chauncey, 88

Bird, Larry, 96

Blair, Bill, 49

Brandon, Terrell, 73, 74

Bryant, Kobe, 5

Bzdelick, Jeff, 103

C

Cassell, Sam, 96, 97, 101, 106, 107, 110

Chamberlain, Wilt, 46, 96, 111

Chicago Bulls, 75

Cleveland, 75

Collins, Doug, 15

D

Dallas Mavericks, 59, 75, 87–89, 90

Dawkins, Darryl, 69

Denver Nuggets, 67, 100–103

DiLeo, Tony, 46

Drexler, Clyde, 59

Duncan, Tim, 67, 74, 83, 92, 96

E

Elie, Mario, 59

F

Fisher, James, 24, 25

Fleisher, Eric, 9, 61

Franks, Baron, 17, 23–24

G

Garnett, Kevin

    All-Star, 55, 76, 92, 93

    arrest, 29–31

    birth of, 18

    declares himself eligible for NBA Draft, 5, 9

    at Farragut Academy, 5, 6, 28, 32, 35

    4XL, 84–87, 108

    named to All-America Team, 7

    named High School Player of the Year, 6

    named Mr. Basketball, 7, 27

    at Mauldin High School, 7, 22, 24–25, 26, 27, 28, 29–31, 38, 50, 51

MVP, 5, 93, 98, 99, 104, 106

number retired, 51

at Olympics, 5, 73–74, 80–81

wins Wooden Award, 7

Garnett, Shirley, 9, 18, 19, 28, 31–33

Gazaway, Darren, 26–27

Gugliotta, Tom, 44, 53, 54, 55, 57, 60, 64, 65, 72

H

Hoiberg, Fred, 96

Hopkins, Stan, 26

Houston Rockets, 59–60, 96

Hudson, Troy, 95

Hurricane Katrina, 108–110

I

Irby, Ernest, 18, 21

J

James, LeBron, 5

Jaric, Marko, 110

Johnson, Magic, 10, 52, 55, 88

Jordan, Michael, 51

L

Laettner, Christian, 44, 49

Long, Murray, 30

Los Angeles Clippers, 98

Los Angeles Lakers, 32, 62, 95–96, 106

M

Madsen, Mark, 96

Malone, Karl, 111

Malone, Moses, 6, 9

Marbury, Stephon, 53–54, 55, 57, 60, 64, 69, 72–73

McCants, Rashad, 110

McCullough, O'Lewis, 18, 21, 109

McDonald's All-American Game, 7

McGrady, Tracy, 5, 92

McHale, Kevin, 15, 37–38, 45, 48, 52, 53–54, 57, 62, 89, 96, 97, 110, 111

Milwaukee, 59, 65, 98

Minnesota Timberwolves

   contract with Kevin Garnett, 38–39, 61–64, 72, 79, 97

   draft Kevin Garnett, 36, 38

Mitchell, Sam, 65–66, 89

N

Nelson, William, 32, 35

New Jersey Nets, 58, 73

O

Olajuwon, Hakeem, 11, 59

Olowokandi, Michael, 96

O'Neal, Jermaine, 5

O'Neal, Shaquille, 62, 99

Oprah Winfrey's Angel Network, 109

Orlando, 76

P

Penny, Romone, 85

Peters, Jamie, 22, 30

Porter, Andrew, 85

Porter, Terry, 64

Portland Trail Blazers, 77, 89, 93

R

Rice, John, 85, 86

Robinson, David, 11, 83

S

Sacramento Kings, 65, 98, 104–106

San Antonio Spurs, 73, 83, 96

Saunders, Flip, 14–15, 49, 52, 75, 89, 105, 106

Sealy, Malik, 24, 75, 77–79, 81

Seattle, 68–71, 72, 75–76

Smith, Joe, 73

Sprewell, Latrell, 96, 97, 101, 107, 110

Stern, David, 9

Szczerbiak, Wally, 74, 88, 104

T

Taylor, Glen, 62, 110

V

Vancouver, 45–46

W

Wallace, Ben, 92

Washington, 51, 58

Willis, Kevin, 59

Willoughby, Bill, 9, 10

Wright, Chris, 85